Rethinking Ownership of Development in Africa

Rethinking Ownership of Development in Africa demonstrates how instead of empowering the communities they work with, the jargon of development ownership often actually serves to perpetuate the centrality of multilateral organizations and international donors in African development, awarding a fairly minimal role to local partners.

In the context of today's development scheme for Africa, ownership is often considered to be the panacea for all of the aid-dependent continent's development woes. Reinforced through the Organization for Economic Co-operation and Development (OECD)'s Paris Declaration on Aid Effectiveness and the Accra Agenda for Action, ownership is now the preeminent procedure for achieving aid effectiveness and a range of development outcomes. Throughout this book, the author illustrates how the ownership paradigm dictates who can produce development knowledge and who is responsible for carrying it out, with a specific focus on the health sectors in Burkina Faso and Kenya. Under this paradigm, despite the ownership narrative, national stakeholders in both countries are not producers of development knowledge; they are merely responsible for its implementation. This book challenges the preponderance of conventional international development policies that call for more ownership from African stakeholders without questioning the implications of donor demands and historical legacies of colonialism in Africa. Ultimately, the findings from this book make an important contribution to critical development debates that question international development as an enterprise capable of empowering developing nations.

This lively and engaging book challenges readers to think differently about the ownership, and as such will be of interest to researchers of development studies and African studies, as well as for development practitioners within Africa.

T. D. Harper-Shipman is an assistant professor of Africana Studies at Davidson College.

Routledge Studies in African Development

Hunger and Poverty in South Africa
The Hidden Faces of Food Insecurity
Jacqueline Hanoman

Extractive Industries and Changing State Dynamics in Africa
Beyond the Resource Curse
Edited by Jon Schubert, Ulf Engel and Elísio Macamo

Peacebuilding in Contemporary Africa
In Search of Alternative Strategies
Edited by Kenneth Omeje

The Challenge of Governance in South Sudan
Corruption, Peacebuilding, and Foreign Intervention
Edited by Steven C. Roach and Derrick K. Hudson

African Peacekeeping Training Centres
Socialisation as a Tool for Peace?
Anne Flaspöler

Corporate Governance in Tanzania
Ethics and Accountability at the Crossroads
Peter C. Mhando

Economic Dualism in Zimbabwe
From Colonial Rhodesia to Post-Independence
Daniel B. Ndlela

Rethinking Ownership of Development in Africa
T.D. Harper-Shipman

Rethinking Ownership of Development in Africa

T. D. Harper-Shipman

Routledge
Taylor & Francis Group

LONDON AND NEW YORK

First published 2020
by Routledge
2 Park Square, Milton Park, Abingdon, Oxon OX14 4RN

and by Routledge
605 Third Avenue, New York, NY 10017

First issued in paperback 2021

Routledge is an imprint of the Taylor & Francis Group, an informa business

British Library Cataloguing-in-Publication Data
A catalogue record for this book is available from the British Library

Library of Congress Cataloging-in-Publication Data
A catalog record for this book has been requested

ISBN 13: 978-0-367-78781-3 (pbk)
ISBN 13: 978-0-367-35290-5 (hbk)

Typeset in Times New Roman
by Apex CoVantage, LLC

I dedicate this book to Cheryl J. Dawkins

Contents

Acknowledgments   viii
List of abbreviations   ix

Introduction   1

1   Theorizing ownership   16

2   La santé avant tout (Health before everything)   41

3   Beggars can't be choosers   67

4   Ownership in comparison   92

Conclusion: Go back and get it   116

Index   125

Acknowledgments

I must acknowledge the Burkinabe and Kenyans who have entrusted me with their words and thoughts. I am grateful for the representatives of the donor organizations who allowed me to quote them on the record. I have to acknowledge the blind reviewers who gave valuable and thought-provoking feedback. The rigorous rounds of reviews, although cumbersome, have made this a much stronger monograph. Thank you to my editor at Routledge, Helena Hurd. I am deeply grateful for your commitment to this project over such a long period of time.

I have to acknowledge my mentors who have been with me at every step of this process: Shareen Hertel, Jane Gordon, Manisha Desai, and Lewis Gordon. You four have helped me navigate and demystify the entire research and writing process. I am forever grateful to you. Dan and Gio, my former colleagues at Carnegie Mellon in the Institute for Politics and Strategy, held me accountable as I reworked various chapters of this book. Kiron Skinner, thank you for creating the space for me and other young scholars to thrive and dedicate much-needed attention to our books. Thank you to my colleagues at Davidson College who have offered various forms of support at different stages: Hilton Kelly, Laurian Bowles, Fuji Lozada, Devyn Benson, and Wendy Raymond. Thank you to Anisha Dhungana, my research assistant.

I don't know how I could have gotten through this process without Meghan Wilson, Aleja Parsons, Jackie Thomas, or Raiki Adams. You all have done everything from keeping my kids to reading terrible drafts of this book while listening to me complain the entire time. Thank you! I want to acknowledge my family, who has always been supportive of my various endeavors (Kaela, I owe you this line!).

To Brandon, Jaelyn, and Yara, you three keep me engaged, loving, and laughing every single day. Brandon, through everything your belief in me as a scholar and force for change has never wavered. You've been my most consistent supporter. Jaelyn and Yara, I'm in awe of you every day. You are precocious, thoughtful, inquisitive, and beautiful girls – please don't ever change.

Abbreviations

CBO	Community-based organization
CDF	Comprehensive Development Framework
CoGes	Comité de Gestion
CSO	Civil Society Organizations
CSPS	Centre de santé et de promotion sociale
DGEP	La Direction Générale de l'Economie et de la Planification (General Directorate for the Economy and Planning)
ERD	External Resource Department
ERSWEC	Economic Recovery Strategy for Wealth and Employment Creation
HIPC	Heavily Indebted Poor Countries
ICPD	International Conference on Population Development
IFI	International Financial Institution
IMF	International Monetary Fund
JICA	Japanese International Co-operation Agency
MCA	Millennium Challenge Accounts
MDGs	Millennium Development Goals
MoFE	Ministry of Finance and Economics
MoH	Ministry of Health
MTEF	Medium Term Expenditure Framework
OECD	Organization for Economic Co-operation and Development
PADS	Programme d'Appui Sanitaire
PNDS	Plan National de Développement Sanitaire
PRSPs	Poverty Reduction Strategy Papers
PTFs	Partenaires Technique et Financier
SAPs	Structural Adjustment Programs
SDGs	Sustainable Development Goals
SIDA	Swedish International Co-operation and Development Agency
SWAp	Sector Wide Approach

UNDP	United Nations Development Programme
UNECA	United Nations Economic Commission for Africa
UNFPA	United Nations Population Fund
USAID	United States Agency for International Development
WHO	World Health Organization

Introduction

The Kenyan Treasury was filled with people as I made my way to my next appointment in the External Resource Department. At that time, in 2013, it was still casually being called the Ministry of Finance. I traipsed down the long corridor until I found the office for my next interview. I was slightly nervous, as a graduate student, coming from the U.S. to Kenya to understand the ubiquitous and somewhat elusive concept of country ownership, ownership of development, or simply ownership in Africa. Much of what I had read at that point described and analyzed ownership as a concept or process that would lead to higher levels of development and lower levels of poverty in African countries receiving aid from the Organization for Economic Co-operation and Development (OECD). The language surrounding ownership also alluded to there being some great shift in traditional development practices between donors and aid recipients. As I softly rapped on the closed office door with the opaque window and waited a few minutes to the sound of nothing, I had a nagging worry that this appointment (like many others) might not happen. As I was about to concede I had been forgotten, she walked up to the door. "Sorry," she said, "I got held up at lunch. Please come in." I walked into a small office made smaller by the large desk and stacks of books and papers. Amidst the clutter, one piece of paper caught my eye. Posted on the wall, as if to serve as a daily reminder, was a plain piece of paper that said, "Donors want government in the driver's seat, but donors want to hold on to the roadmap." The researcher in me was reinvigorated. I had seen and heard the trope that informed the sign: Ownership means that governments are in the driver's seat, but this was the first time that I had seen it reconfigured to suggest that not much has changed with the advent of ownership. Thinking that seeing the sign in her office was surely an indication that we could have a frank conversation about ownership, I asked her, "Did you put this paper up?" "Huh?" she asked, as she continued to settle into her office. I pointed to the paper and asked again.

"Oh, no," she stated, almost as if she was unaware that the paper was even there. "That was there when I moved into this office. So, what is it you're doing in Kenya?"

This book is about power, development, and ideas in the health sectors of two African countries: Burkina Faso and Kenya. I examine these phenomena in the context of ownership. The OECD defines ownership as "a developing country government's abilities to exercise leadership over their development policies and strategies and co-ordinate development actions" (OECD 2011, 29).[1] The demand for more country ownership in African countries receiving aid from the OECD Development Assistance Committee (OECD-DAC) is now pervasive. Both multilateral and bilateral development institutions have used ownership to explain successes in developing African countries. For example, in an article on why Africa has failed to industrialize, the United Nations (UN) explained,

> Ethiopia, Rwanda and to a lesser extent Tanzania have proved adept at navigating the bumpy path to industrialization. The common thread among them is that they have embraced policies that target and favour their own manufacturing industries. . . . And most importantly, they have shown a commitment to and *ownership* of these policies.
>
> (Tafirenyika 2016)

Throughout this book, I argue that the putative version of ownership in contemporary development discourse is distinct from previous renderings of ownership because the current version is better understood as a development paradigm. The language and practice needed to demonstrate this type of ownership does not automatically translate into more control and independence for some aid-receiving African countries. Based on two case studies, Burkina Faso and Kenya, I find that ownership dictates the acceptable tools, actors, problems, ideas, and discourses that Burkinabe and Kenyan actors must engage if they are to demonstrate that they are owning their development processes. In this form, ownership can constrain or empower local stakeholders in their quests to define and achieve social and economic progress.

This ownership paradigm further entrenches donors in the decision-making apparatus and reinforces donors as development experts.[2] Although donors maintain considerable influence over policy with their "expertise," there is little to no mutual accountability, as the Burkinabe and Kenyan governments assume full responsibility for unsuccessful policies. These findings are of paramount importance because they indicate a pressing need to rethink what we mean by "country ownership" or "ownership of development" when advocating for changes in development practices in aid-receiving African countries. In lieu of demanding that these countries "own" development and all that it entails, practitioners and scholars interested in country-specific and country-led renderings of and strategies for progress should consider moving beyond the ownership discourse.

This book probes two questions: What is ownership of development, and how do local stakeholders in different African countries define and navigate ownership? I sought to answer these questions in two disparate African countries – Burkina Faso and Kenya. In both countries, I used the health sector as a contextual anchor for exploring how civil society actors, donors, and government officials negotiate and navigate owning development. Months of fieldwork in both countries culminated in seventy-five semi-structured interviews and participant observations that I triangulated across policy documents from all three groups in each country. These data point to a hegemonic version of ownership that is operating in tandem with some historical and country-informed versions of ownership in Burkina Faso and Kenya. I identify two mechanisms: Trust, in the Kenyan case, and professionalization, in the Burkinabe case. Trust and professionalization are not unintended consequences detached from the larger matrix of ownership in either case. Both mechanisms maintain the existing power relations between donors and local stakeholders while incrementally altering the social institutions that impede a pervasive and profound adoption of country-specific development.

In this book, I will show how Kenya, which has garnered a reputation for being hostile to ownership and reforms, does, in fact, demonstrate commitment to owning development, albeit in ways that give the government leverage vis-à-vis donors not only at the level of policy adoption and implementation but also in an unwavering commitment to the ownership discourse and belief in the associated tools. In doing so, the Kenyan government uses their commitment to the ownership paradigm to "reestablish" trust, disassociate itself from the donor community, and demonstrate that they are also "knowers" of development. In Burkina Faso, community-based organizations (CBOs) work in their respective communities to improve community health outcomes. Limited avenues for independent funding force many of the CBOs to appeal to other stakeholders specifically non-governmental organizations (NGOs), donors, and the Burkinabe government to finance their activities. The funding that the CBOs receive from the other stakeholders is allocated based on the country's national development strategy and health sector strategy. In order to access these funds, the CBOs must reconfigure aspects of their missions and approaches to community to health so that the organizations remain legible and useful to the other three stakeholders. Being professionalized in accordance with the larger ownership discourse means that the CBOs must orient their work towards collecting data towards the broader focus on results-based development.

My time spent as a community health volunteer in Peace Corps Burkina Faso from 2010 until 2012 colors my analysis of ownership. My reasons for joining the Peace Corps unfortunately aligned with my community's perception of my role during those two years – to fix their problems. Only, I had miscalculated the problem. The longer I immersed myself in the community, the more I realized that my position as a Volunteer framed me as a development expert, when in reality, I was merely an interlocutor for some people in the community to navigate culturally-specific development language and tools so that they might access resources that were otherwise unavailable to them. I, in fact, was no expert but a privileged part of a culture and system that created the rules for the hegemonic notions of "development" (Zein-Elabdin 2016).

Ownership: A brief history

Demands for more state-led development across Sub-Saharan Africa date back to the 1950s and 1960s with the end of the formal period of European colonization. African leaders like Julius Nyerere and Kwame NKrumah were at the forefront of regional and global movements in the South to reconfigure the international economic order in such a way that nascent states in Africa, Asia, and Latin America could effectively develop their countries and build state-level capacity (Prashad 2014; Ibhawoh and Dibua 2003; Nkrumah 1968). Part of reconfiguring the so-called Third World was demanding both domestic-level policy space and the global economic resources to own national development. Leaders from the Third World were not the only ones referring to ownership in the 1960s. Former World Bank President Robert McNamara commissioned an investigation to determine the effectiveness of World Bank aid and recommend improvements based on the Pearson Commission. The Pearson Commission on International Development published its findings in a report titled *Partners in Development*. One of the many findings was a need to better incorporate other voices and actors into the aid relationship, beyond just donors and aid-receiving governments (World Bank 2003). Aspects of ownership have always been a part of the international aid architecture. It is, however, the unique packaging of assumptions, expectations, tools, language, and practices that make the current form of ownership different from previous calls for government-led development.

Specific reference to the word *ownership* was prominent in the 1990s. More precisely, the World Bank (the Bank) began referring to "ownership of structural adjustments" as an ideal framework for aid-receiving countries to commit to structural adjustment policies (Johnson and Wasty 1993; Mosley, Harrigan, and Toye 1995). In this form, governments receiving adjustment loans from the Bank and the International Monetary Fund (IMF) would demonstrate ownership by following through on the conditionalities attached to the adjustment loans (Johnson and Wasty 1993). The economic policies that the Bank and IMF required aid-receiving governments to own came under intense scrutiny towards the end of the decade. Activists around the world led protests against the neoliberal economic policies that characterized the Bretton Woods institutions' reforms (Broad 2002). Eventually, critiques of the Bank and IMF began to come directly from American policymakers in Washington. For example, the Bush administration tried to defund the World Bank and began giving more leverage to bilateral development interventions through the U.S. Agency for International Development (USAID) and the Millennium Challenge Accounts (MCA) to promote neoliberal policies (Engler 2011). Both the World Bank and the IMF experienced a crisis of legitimacy as institutions and required public facelifts (Kosack, Ranis, and Vreeland 2004; Stone 2011). The Bank responded to the global critiques with the Comprehensive Development Framework (CDF) as indication of a change in its development approach. The CDF promoted country-led development through the use of Bank and IMF-approved development strategies, partnership across various stakeholders, like civil society and the private sector, and a focus on measurable results (Wolfensohn and Fischer 2000). It was through the CDF that Poverty Reduction Strategy Papers (PRSPs) were linked as requisite tools for ownership (Harper-Shipman 2019).

Other international institutions began incorporating the CDF brand of ownership in the early 2000s into their strategies for improving aid effectiveness, development cooperation, and achieving the Millennium Development Goals (MDGs). For example, in 2002, the UN hosted the International Conference on Financing for Development, in Monterrey, Mexico. Collaborating to fund development and eradicate poverty, the conference participants (composed of heads of states from across the globe) identified "national leadership and ownership of development" as necessary for successful partnership among recipient countries and donors (United Nations 2002, 14). In 2003, in response to mounting criticism of foreign aid's inability to produce its intended aims – poverty reduction – the OECD began a series of high-level forums to discuss increasing the effectiveness of foreign aid (Easterly and Williamson 2011; Moyo 2009). The four OECD high-level fora, which took place in Rome (2003), Paris (2005), Accra (2008), and Busan (2011), established a set of principles for ameliorating aid practices, including donor-government relations, in efforts to reach the MDGs.

The first meeting in Rome produced the Rome Declaration on Harmonization, which reaffirmed the commitments outlined in the Monterrey

Consensus. The meeting in Rome also gave considerable import to the task of harmonizing development assistance at the country level. The 2005 meeting in Paris was perhaps the most notable, in that the Paris Declaration on Aid Effectiveness emerged from that forum. This document articulates the five principles for improving aid effectiveness: Ownership, alignment, harmonization, results, and mutual accountability (Paris Declaration 2012). Alignment aims to redress donors' inconsistent use of country systems and institutions to deliver aid by aligning with country priorities to simultaneously strengthen domestic systems and institutions. Harmonization is an effort to reduce duplicate projects and waste across donors and funding. By harmonizing donors, the assumption is that national governments will avoid the burden of dealing with multiple procedures and demands from a wide range of donors, which requires a mobilization of resources for each encounter. The focus on being result-oriented means elaborating domestic mechanisms for measuring achievement of national development strategies and international benchmarks, like MDGs. Mutual accountability refers to governments and donors establishing transparency around the usage of public funds domestically and abroad, respectively (OECD 2011, 85). Accountability was also meant to dis-incentivize governments from engaging in corrupt practices. In line with the CDF structure, ownership is the pinnacle of the aid-effectiveness pyramid.

International stakeholders found that definition of ownership coming out of the Paris Declaration was not capacious enough – more than just aid-receiving governments could and should own their development processes. These sentiments were salient in the 2008 High Level Meeting in Accra. The Accra Agenda for Action (AAA) brought back to the fore the importance of non-government stakeholders for successful ownership. The final High Level meeting took place in Busan, Korea, in 2011, where once again, promoting the necessity of country ownership for achieving increased aid effectiveness and improving stakeholder partnerships were at the forefront of the agenda. The Busan Partnership for Effective Development Cooperation reinforced the relationship among ownership, transparency, partnership, and results for improving development cooperation, which would ideally translate into greater poverty reduction.

Paradigmatic ownership

In 2018, at the London School of Economics, current World Bank President, Jim Yong Kim opined:

> But let me be clear – this isn't like the bad old days of privatization. I was part of a group that protested those bad old days. We're not

talking about reviving an approach where the answer to poorly run public services, or unprofitable state-owned enterprises, was often an over-simplified attempt at privatization. . . . We're talking about a very different kind of approach. What emerged from Addis Ababa was a consensus that private capital was essential for development – but that development had to be country-led and always focused on benefitting the poor.

(Kim 2018)

In this speech, Kim reproduces the broadly accepted narrative that the Bank and other donors, which were responsible for enforcing a series of market-driven policies and political conditionalities that reconfigured the role of the state to be in service of the market (otherwise known as neoliberalism), are now doing something different. The Bank, especially, now realizes that the state is important. However, the state must now take steps to own development in such a way that public-private partnership can flourish. Kim is articulating and promoting the ownership paradigm.[3]

Starting with the call for ownership of structural adjustments in the 1990s and moving through the CDF, Monterrey Consensus, and OECD high level forums ownership became more than just a buzzword. These different international institutions collaborated on a set of tools, language, and practice that if absent from domestic-level development strategizing would indicate something other than ownership. In this book, I focus on three requisite tools for ownership: Poverty Reduction Strategy Papers (PRSPs), Sector Wide Approach (SWAp), and Medium-Term Expenditure Framework (MTEF). PRSPs are the long-term, comprehensive, collaborative, results-oriented development strategies that all countries wishing to receive concessional loans from the Bank must produce. Countries produced interim PRSPs as qualifying-round outlines of their strategies. Once the IMF and Bank approved the interim PRSPs, countries could resume receipt of the Poverty Reduction and Growth Facility, previously called the Enhanced Structural Adjustment Facility. Part of the requirements was the adoption of the other institutional frameworks, the SWAp and MTEF.

The MTEF is a three- to five-year planning strategy that identifies development priorities from the PRSP and outlines clear constraints and expectations for financing those priorities. It is the budget management tool for the PRSPs. The MTEF is key in that it specifies the financial dimensions of the thirty-year development strategy in shorter time-spans. In a 2013 report on MTEFs, the Bank states that the goal is for MTEFs to replace annual budgeting (HLSP Insitute 2005). "Donors played an important role in encouraging the implementation of MTEFs [in Africa]. Part of their motivation was to improve public financial management as a means to ensure that external assistance and domestic resources would support development programs directed toward poverty alleviation" (HLSP Insitute 2005, 10). SWAps, theoretically, coordinate programs tied to the MTEF, making aid more effective and efficient (HLSP Insitute 2005). Participating African governments striving for ownership elaborate, in conjunction with donors, SWAPs and MTEFs based on the PRSP, which should broaden national ownership (HLSP 2005). Each sector drafts its own development strategy with clear priorities, ownership, broad stakeholder collaboration, etc. The MTEF and SWAp are considered essential tools for achieving ownership because they aid in the implementation of pro-poor policies.

Beyond the application of these tools, stakeholders must also master and incorporate a discourse informed by the ownership paradigm. By discourse, I am referring to the ideational, linguistic, and practical structures that, combined, imply relations of power. Discourses specify who and what can be said, who are the relevant actors, and what their roles are (Hall 2006; Carant 2017; Fairclough 2013). There has been much discussion about a "development discourse," especially in the post-development literature (Andrews and Bawa 2014; Matthews 2017; Parfitt 2011; Escobar 1995). Under the ownership paradigm, there exist unique discourses, such as partnership, knowledge experts, mutual accountability, and results, that work collectively to delineate the contours of ownership. These, and other discourses, signal to all development stakeholders their responsibilities, acceptable goals, which results matter, which do not, who is an expert, and who is not. Some might argue that some of these discourses are not new; they have been around in various forms since the 1960s, at least. Such an observation would be correct, but as Stuart Hall explains, "Discourses are not closed systems. A discourse draws on elements in other discourse, binding them into its own network of meaning" (Hall 2006, 202). This book explores the network of meaning that emanates from the global call for more ownership. I trace and articulate how development actors, specifically those understood as donors, government officials, and civil society members, navigate, adopt, reject, and/or negotiate the ownership discourse in Burkina Faso and Kenya.

Understanding ownership as a paradigm distinguishes it from other expressions of ownership or how other African countries control their development. Okereke and Agupusi highlight this distinction in Africa by focusing on homegrown development approaches. Homegrown development also gives primacy to "who controls the ideas and development processes," by centering local actors and the initiatives particular to their contexts as the strategy (2015, 31). For an approach to be homegrown, there can be no external conditionalities. Ownership may or may not be a corollary of a homegrown approach. Okereke and Agupusi argue that it is possible to have ownership in the dominant sense *without* producing a homegrown strategy because ownership does not refer to "total independence or autonomy of borrowing countries over their development policies and programmes" (2015, 33). They provide an example from the United Nations Economic Commission for Africa (UNECA), which states that ownership is "a set of relationships between Africa and international partners in which each will hold the other accountable for overall performance towards mutually-agreed development outcomes." African governments must "*adhere to agreed principles of governance and . . . meet criteria for sound public finance management*" (UNECA 2001, 31, as cited in Okereke and Agupusi 2015, 34; emphasis mine). This distinction further highlights the difference between what I term the ownership paradigm and other configurations of ownership. The paradigmatic version of ownership necessitates donor participation, while homegrown approaches almost require the absence of donor involvement.

The stakeholders

As I noted previously, ownership as a paradigm identifies the necessary development actors and their roles in bringing about development. These actors are referred to as stakeholders – the social, political, and economic groups that have a vested interest in national development. Many of these actors can be grouped into categories based on their ability to shape and direct policies. Governments, donors, and civil society organizations (CSOs) are the three primary stakeholders that I examine in the Kenyan and Burkinabe health sectors.

The government is the primary owner of development. This role, however, is complicated in many African contexts because development scholarship generally casts African states as antithetical to development. In much of the contemporary development literature, the *African state* is interchangeable with neopatrimonial, failed, predatory, or simply not working (Hyden 2005; Bates, Coatsworth, and Williamson 2007; Mkandawire 2015; Mills et al. 2017). The pejorative view of governance in Africa informs how the ownership paradigm frames the responsibilities of the state and other actors in many African contexts. One of the more prominent consequences of this view is that many African states are not yet capable of owning development because they do not have the institutional capacity or political will power (Booth 2012; Faust 2010). The Kenyan case study further illustrates how ownership has little to do with a state actually leading in the ways that they deem best and more to do with following a prescribed formula for a particular type of governance structure.

CSOs are the other crucial actors for ownership. Dominant theorizations of civil society define civil society as a distinct sphere that exists independent of the state and the market; this autonomy allows civil society actors to regulate and place checks on political and economic institutions, keeping them from becoming hegemonic (Edwards 2009; Fukuyama 2001; Polanyi 2001). Development discourse, and thus the ownership paradigm, fully incorporates this understanding of civil society into its schema (Steinle and Correll 2008; World Bank 2000; Paris Declaration 2012; Wood et al. 2008; Fisher and Marquette 2016). The ownership paradigm furthers a benevolent rendering of civil society and, more specifically, NGOs, as they are responsible for carrying out development programs and delivering services while acting as the watchdogs for donors trying to will governments to comply with conditionalities (Mundy et al. 2007, 2). Because the ownership paradigm heavily implicates civil society in the development process, I interviewed representatives from civil society organizations such as NGOs and CBOs. I was able to observe meetings between representatives from the local health associations of Tenkodogo, Burkina Faso, and their funding NGO regarding local efforts to implement the health sector strategy. Examining the sphere of civil society allowed me to discern the ways in which ownership percolates through to the everyday activities of CSO actors. Including a focus on civil society actors in Burkina Faso and Kenya also highlights the need to abandon the assumption that power dynamics in the aid architecture can only be observed between the donors and the state. Unpacking and analyzing the ways in which civil society organizations navigate donors and the state and adopt or reject development discourses should be standard in any analysis of development in Africa.

Under the ownership paradigm, donors are partners that offer financial and technical expertise. They are responsible for building capacity in aid-receiving countries by providing governments with the skills and knowledge to build effective institutions for sustainable development. Framing donors as experts makes the hubristic assumption that donors are, in fact, experts. This framing also assumes that donors are always benevolent actors. In this way, development in many aid-receiving African countries becomes an un-reflexive narrative of the benevolent donor fighting for (and sometimes with) civil society organizations against the malignant African state for progress. For example, Pablo Yanguas' fascinating book, *Why We Lie About Aid*, positions donors, or as he calls them, challengers, as constantly pushing to implement change (2018, 186). He states, "External ideas – such as 'good governance', participation and adaptation are used by challengers as a springboard for initiating processes of change" (2018, 188). Yanguas inadvertently lapses into the problematic that he seeks to subvert, proposing a simplified view of development and its actors. Implicit in his empirics and anecdotes is the donors-are-good and local-stakeholders-are-bad narrative. To use Yanguas's nomenclature, donors are not always challengers, and governments and other local stakeholders are not always incumbents. Nevertheless, donors as challengers, experts, and/or partners in domestic-level processes towards ownership is an important discourse in the ownership paradigm. This troubled dynamic is especially salient when local actors are included in the analysis and when we focus on the discursive elements of aid. In this book, I want to highlight how within these very powerful donor organizations, there are actors trying to implement change in recipient countries according to what they believe is sound evidence, even if that evidence is impervious to criticism from other stakeholders.

Decolonize ownership

Based on my interrogation of how donors, civil society actors, and government officials adopt, manipulate, and/or reject ownership discourses to advance their own notions of development, I argue that ownership, with all its trappings, must be decolonized in language and in practice. In order for ownership to create the much-needed space wherein Burkinabe and Kenyan stakeholders can imagine versions of progress that speak to the myriad contexts in each country, we must first "rethink" and begin "unthinking" ownership (Wallerstein 1991; Ndlovu-Gatsheni 2013, 84). Decolonial theory provides both a critical and generative response to the limitations of the ownership paradigm as it continues to reinforce and support a privileged interpretation and development practice in Burkina Faso and Kenya.

The decolonial school of thought explores, among other things, how knowledge production is concomitant with geopolitical contexts (Graham 2014; Mignolo 2009; Ndlovu-Gatsheni 2015). Decolonial theory asks, "Who and when, why and where is knowledge generated" (Mignolo 2009, 160)? Analyzing for whom ownership was created, the historical factors that necessitated the need for such a paradigm, and the geopolitical terrain that informed its discourses (i.e. technical experts, good governance, and capacity building) illuminates webs of power relations based on antiquated hierarchies of development knowledge (Cooke 2003). If development practitioners and scholars in Africa envisage a continent where countries are in the drivers' seats, then these countries must have the space to imagine the terrain and design the road map, or simply burn the map.

Structure of the book

Chapter one delves deeper into the theoretical framework, decolonial theory, and its import for understanding and advancing ownership in both countries. It also provides an overview of the current literature on ownership, in which I argue that ownership is best explored from an ideational perspective. Chapter two presents the first empirical case study, Burkina Faso, in which all development stakeholders have fully adopted the ownership principles under the pretense of there being a Faustian-type bargain between the government and donors. Although the government and civil society organizations recognize that donors continue to heavily influence the country's development trajectory, Burkinabe stakeholders view themselves as underdeveloped and lacking the necessary resources to reach development. Donors, although intrusive, provide Burkina with the necessary epistemic and financial resources to achieve development. The Burkina Faso case also demonstrates how the ownership paradigm constrains development choices at the local level.

Chapter three concerns Kenya, the second empirical case of an African country that has taken up the ownership paradigm for its development ends. The Kenyan government, although displaying a mastery of the development lexis and an expressed commitment to the principles, remains in a paternalistic relationship with donors. Donors believe that the Kenyan government does not own development because the government refuses to follow up with implementation. Instead of viewing the lack of implementation as demonstrative of flaws in the ownership paradigm, donors view it as emblematic of a longer history of poor governance in Kenya. The fourth chapter comparatively analyzes the findings from the two case studies, exploring explores the construction of donors as experts and the absolution of donors from any responsibility for development failures. Chapter four also explores the different conceptualizations of ownership that come from both countries and offers an historical institutionalist explanation for their divergence.

Notes

1 I do not include non-OECD donors for two key reasons: One, non-OECD countries are not signatory to this brand of ownership, meaning they may or may not have the same stance regarding aid and ownership as OECD countries; and two, OECD countries were the largest contributors to the health sectors in the two countries used in this study.

2 I am aware that the term "donors" is no longer widely accepted in development literature. The more favorable term, which coincides with ostensible changes in development practices is "development partners."

3 By referring to ownership as a paradigm, I am arguing that there is a range of relatively consistent ideas, methods, theories, commitments, approaches, and beliefs that together construct a particular reality associated with ownership as a model for development (Geddes 2003; Kuhn 2012). According to Geddes, paradigms determine "which facts are theoretically salient; defining what constitutes a paradox and what questions urgently require answers; identifying which cases need to be examined and what kinds of evidence are considered meaningful" (2003, 7).

References

Andrews, Nathan, and Sylvia Bawa. 2014. "A Post-Development Hoax? (Re)-Examining the Past, Present and Future of Development Studies." *Third World Quarterly* 35 (6): 922–38.

Bates, Robert, John Coatsworth, and Jeffrey Williamson. 2007. "Lost Decades: Postindependence Performance in Latin America and Africa." *The Journal of Economic History* 67 (4): 917.

Booth, David. 2012. "Aid Effectiveness: Bringing Country Ownership (and Politics) Back In." *Conflict, Security & Development* 12 (5): 537–58.

Broad, Robin. 2002. *Global Backlash: Citizen Initiatives for a Just World Economy.* Lanham, MD: Rowman & Littlefield.

Carant, Jane Briant. 2017. "Unheard Voices: A Critical Discourse Analysis of the Millennium Development Goals' Evolution into the Sustainable Development Goals." *Third World Quarterly* 38 (1): 1–26.

Cooke, Bill. 2003. "A New Continuity with Colonial Administration: Participation in Development Management." *Third World Quarterly* 24 (1): 47–61.

Easterly, William, and Claudia R. Williamson. 2011. "Rhetoric versus Reality: The Best and Worst of Aid Agency Practices." *World Development* 39 (11): 1930–49.

Edwards, Michael. 2009. *Civil Society.* Cambridge: Polity Press.

Engler, Mark. 2011. "Abandoning the World Bank: Pitfalls When Right and Left Agree." *Dissent* 53 (4): 57–63.

Escobar, Arturo. 1995. *Encountering Development: The Making and Unmaking of the Third World.* Princeton, NJ: Princeton University Press.

Fairclough, Norman. 2013. "Critical Discourse Analysis and Critical Policy Studies." *Critical Policy Studies* 7 (2): 177–97.

Faust, Jörg. 2010. "Policy Experiments, Democratic Ownership and Development Assistance." *Development Policy Review* 28 (5): 515–34.

Fisher, Jonathan, and Heather Marquette. 2016. "'Empowered Patient' or 'Doctor Knows Best'? Political Economy Analysis and Ownership." *Development in Practice* 26 (1): 115–26.

Fukuyama, Francis. 2001. "Social Capital, Civil Society and Development." *Third World Quarterly* 22 (1): 7–20.

Geddes, Barbara. 2003. *Paradigms and Sand Castles: Theory Building and Research Design in Comparative Politics.* Ann Arbor: University of Michigan Press.

Graham, James. 2014. "Decoloniality and Development." *Journal of Southern African Studies* 40 (4): 891–93.

Hall, Stuart. 2006. "The West and the Rest: Discourse and Power." In *The Indigenous Experience: Global Perspectives*, edited by Roger Maaka and Chris Andersen, 165–73. Ontario: Canadian Scholars' Press.

Harper-Shipman, T. D. 2019. "How Comprehensive is Comprehensive? Using Wangari Maathai as a Critique of the World Bank's Contemporary Development Model." *Third World Quarterly.*

HLSP Insitute. 2005. "Sector Wide Approaches: A Resource Document for UNFPA Staff." Accessed April 24, 2019. www.unfpa.org/sites/default/files/pub-pdf/swap-unfpa2005eng.pdf.

Hyden, Goran. 2005. *African Politics in Comparative Perspective*. Cambridge and New York: Cambridge University Press.

Ibhawoh, Bonny, and J. I. Dibua. 2003. "Deconstructing Ujamaa: The Legacy of Julius Nyerere in the Quest for Social and Economic Development in Africa." *African Journal of Political Science* 8 (1): 59–83.

Johnson, John H., and Sulaiman S. Wasty. 1993. *Borrower Ownership of Adjustment Programs and the Political Economy of Reform*. Vol. 199. Washington, DC: World Bank Publications.

Kim, Jim Yong. 2018. "In Senegal, a Call to Invest in People and the Planet." only. The World Bank Voices. February 21, 2018. Accessed April 24, 2019. https://blogs.worldbank.org/voices/senegal-invest-people-planet.

Kosack, Stephen, Gustav Ranis, and James Vreeland, eds. 2004. *Globalization and the Nation State: The Impact of the IMF and the World Bank*. Abingdon: Routledge.

Kuhn, Thomas S. 2012. *The Structure of Scientific Revolutions: 50th Anniversary Edition*. Chicago: University of Chicago Press.

Matthews, Sally. 2017. "Colonised Minds? Post-Development Theory and the Desirability of Development in Africa." *Third World Quarterly* 38 (12): 2650–63.

Mignolo, Walter. 2009. "Epistemic Disobedience, Independent Thought and Decolonial Freedom." *Theory, Culture & Society* 26 (7–8): 159–81.

Mills, Greg, Olusegun Obasanjo, Jeffrey Herbst, and Dickie Davis. 2017. *Making Africa Work: A Handbook*. 1 edition. London: Hurst.

Mkandawire, Thandika. 2015. "Neopatrimonialism and the Political Economy of Economic Performance in Africa: Critical Reflections." *World Politics* 67 (3).

Mosley, Paul, Jane Harrigan, and John Toye. 1995. *Aid and Power: The World Bank and Policy-Based Lending. Volume 1: Analysis and Policy Proposals*. 2nd ed. Abingdon: Routledge.

Moyo, Dambisa. 2009. *Dead Aid: Why Aid Is Not Working and How There Is a Better Way for Africa*. London: Macmillan.

Mundy, Karen, Suzanne Cherry, Megan Haggerty, Richard Maclure, and Malini Sivasubramaniam. 2007. *Basic Education, Civil Society Participation and the New Aid Architecture: Lessons from Burkina Faso, Kenya, Mali and Tanzania*. Toronto: University of Toronto, Comparative and International Development Centre.

Ndlovu-Gatsheni, Sabelo J. 2013. *Empire, Global Coloniality and African Subjectivity*. New York: Berghahn Books.

———. 2015. "Decoloniality as the Future of Africa." *History Compass* 13 (10): 485–96.

Nkrumah, Kwame. 1968. *Neo-Colonialism: The Last Stage of Imperialism*. London: Panaf Books.

OECD. 2011. *Aid Effectiveness 2005–10: Progress in Implementing the Paris Declaration*. Paris: OECD Publishing.

Okereke, Chukwumerije, and Patricia Agupusi. 2015. *Homegrown Development in Africa: Reality or Illusion?* Abingdon: Routledge.

Parfitt, Trevor. 2011. "Post-Development and Its Discontents." *Journal of Critical Realism* 10 (4): 442–64.

Paris Declaration. 2012. "Accra Agenda for Action." Paris: OECD. www.oecd.org/dac/effectiveness/34428351.pdf.

Polanyi, Karl. 2001. *The Great Transformation: The Political and Economic Origins of Our Time*. Boston, MA: Beacon Press.

Prashad, Vijay. 2014. *The Poorer Nations: A Possible History of the Global South by Vijay Prashad*. New York: Verso Books.

Steinle, Aurora, and Denys Correll. 2008. *Can Aid Be Effective Without Civil Society? The Paris Declaration, the Accra Agenda for Action and Beyond*. Bronx, NY: International Council on Social Welfare (ICSW).

Stone, Randall W. 2011. *Controlling Institutions: International Organizations and the Global Economy*. Cambridge: Cambridge University Press.

Tafirenyika, Masimba. 2016. "Why Has Africa Failed to Industrialize? Africa Renewal Online." Africa Renewal. August 2016. www.un.org/africarenewal/magazine/august-2016/why-has-africa-failed-industrialize.

United Nations. 2002. *Monterrey Consensus on Financing for Development*. New York: United Nations Department of Economic and Social Affairs.

Wallerstein, Immanuel Maurice. 1991. *Unthinking Social Science: The Limits of Nineteenth-Century Paradigms*. Cambridge: Polity Press.

Wolfensohn, James D., and Stanley Fischer. 2000. "The Comprehensive Development Framework (CDF) and Poverty Reduction Strategy Papers (PRSP): Joint Note by James D. Wolfensohn and Stanley Fischer." www.imf.org/external/np/prsp/pdf/cdfprsp.pdf.

Wood, Bernard, Dorte Kabell, Nansozi Muwanga, and Francisco Sagasti. 2008. "Evaluation of the Implementation of the Paris Declaration: Phase One: Synthesis Report." Ministry of Foreign Affairs of Denmark. www.oecd.org/derec/dacnetwork/40900736.pdf.

World Bank. 2000. *Attacking Poverty*. Edited by S. M. Ravi Kanbur and Nora Lustig. World Development Report, 2000/2001. New York: Published for the World Bank, Oxford University Press.

———. 2003. "World Bank Group Archives: The Pearson Commission." Number 030. Exhibit Series. Washington, DC: The World Bank Group.

Yanguas, Pablo. 2018. *Why We Lie about Aid*. London: Zed Books.

Zein-Elabdin, Eiman. 2016. *Economics, Culture and Development*. London: Routledge.

1   Theorizing ownership

In 2011, then-Secretary of State Hillary Clinton delivered a speech in Busan, Korea, on U.S. support for the current aid architecture. In this speech, Secretary Clinton candidly promoted the need for ownership, stating,

> We need to get serious about what we mean when we talk about country ownership of development strategies. Let's be clear, too often, donors' decisions are driven more by our own political interests or our policy preferences or development orthodoxies than by our partners' needs. But now our partners have access to evidence-based analysis and best practices, so they can better decide what will work for them. We have to be willing to follow their lead.
>
> (United States Government 2012, 5)

Five years later, at the United Nations, while speaking on the significance of the new Sustainable Development Goals (SDGs) in Africa, the Administrator of the United Nation's Development Programme (UNDP), Helen Clark, noted,

> Broad coalitions around the SDGs are needed to leverage stakeholders' strengths, build synergies, and promote *national ownership*. Government leadership and commitment to the SDGs is vital, but it is insufficient on its own. To achieve the SDGs, there will need to be engagement across civil society, the private sector, philanthropy, multilateral institutions, and development partners as appropriate.
>
> (Clark 2016, n.p.; emphasis mine)

These two statements encapsulate the appeal and parameters of ownership. At face value, a figure as notable as Hillary Clinton endorsing and demanding that donors allow government to lead seems to promote a rupture in the traditional power dynamics that characterized aid relationships in the

1980s and 1990s. And, if, as Clark explained, ownership is compulsory for achieving the SDGs, then how could the utility of ownership be in question? In fact, wouldn't moving beyond ownership be counterproductive? A closer examination of Clinton's statement exposes the conditions that ownership imposes on aid-receiving countries – governments must be equipped with evidence-based analyses and best practices before they are ready to own development. It is through exploration of these types of discourses that are internal to the ownership paradigm that the remnants of coloniality are most evident.

Decolonize ownership

Decolonial political economy allows us to map the contours of ownership as another mechanism of coloniality in development discourse (Keita 2011; Zein-Elabdin 2001). By coloniality, I am referring to the language and practice that mirror and are legacies of colonial relations in this so-called postcolonial moment (Mignolo 2009; Grosfoguel 2007; Maldonado-Torres 2007; Ndlovu-Gatsheni 2015). Coloniality better explains why, in the ownership literature, scholars find that donors are unwilling to fully concede control over development policy formulation and project design to governments and local communities in the global south. Donors' use of the ownership discourse *ipso facto* re-inscribes power relations that do not require them to abdicate their long-held epistemic and financial control. Quijano (2007) proposes four critical spaces of coloniality: control over the economy, authority, gender and sexuality, and knowledge and subjectivity. Using decolonial political economy to understand ownership in Burkina Faso and Kenya exposes how and why the language of poor governance does not fully capture the reasons for mistrust between donors and governments. Coloniality also better explains why donors, although embedded in the governing apparatus and civil society as epistemic and financial actors, are not held accountable for poverty and policy failures. The development economics that inform the "expertise" that donors provide to governments and NGOs is imbued with power that recreates subjugated knowledges organized around culturally based epistemics encapsulated in what James Ferguson (2006) calls "scientific capitalism."

Scientific capitalism refers to the presentation of "neutral, technical principles of efficiency and pragmatism" as solutions to public policy divorced from any specific moral order, when, in reality,

> a whole set of moral premises are implicit in these technicizing arguments. Notions of the inviolate rights of individuals, the sanctity of private property, the nobility of capitalist accumulation, and the intrinsic

value of 'freedom' (understood as the freedom to engage in economic transactions) lie just below the surface.

(Ferguson 2006, 80)

In Burkina Faso and Kenya, scientific capitalism constructs Burkinabe and Kenyan stakeholders as possessing only "local" knowledge that acts to increase the effectiveness of the capacity building and technical expertise that donors provide. I demonstrate how Burkinabe and Kenyan stakeholders at times contest these boundaries, while at other times they willingly reproduce them in the interest of development. Scientific capitalism is also maintained on the assumption that aid's ineffectiveness, corruption, and poverty levels are in no way tied to donor actions (Escobar 1995; W. Sachs 1992; Quan 2012). Again, decoloniality of knowledge and power centers the experiences and concerns of Kenyan and Burkinabe stakeholders as necessary for understanding the potential and limitations of ownership. Doing so points to the ways in which ownership has done little to decolonize or alter the relations of power and conceptions of knowledge around development in either country (Maldonado-Torres 2007). It exposes how concepts like governance and mutual accountability, although deployed under ostensibly benevolent terms, are essential in maintaining an aid environment where the full range of actors responsible for poverty and corruption continues to elude responsibility.

My aim is to demonstrate, based on seventy-five interviews across the health sectors of two very different African countries, how the ownership paradigm that is so heavily promoted as the panacea to economic, social, and political quandaries in much of Africa, may have more elements of the traditional donor-government interactions embedded in its design than development scholars are willing to admit. A change in the methodological analysis and focus on community-level stakeholders present an indisputable picture of local actors in these two countries navigating a web of restraints and elusive footholds as knowers of development. Where scholars and practitioners have explored the question and parameters of ownership, they have focused almost exclusively on donor-government relations. Very little scholarship looks at ownership in civil society, and those examples do not address Africa (Buffardi 2013; Meyer and Schulz 2008). Along with the exclusion of civil society from the analysis, there has been no genuine interrogation of how stakeholders are actually defining and interacting with the paradigm. Are all development stakeholders operating with the same conceptualizations and understandings of what it means to "own development"? How are actors using the institutions and byproducts of ownership to achieve their own unique development ends? What informs the language and desire for ownership in its current form? I argue, based on an excavation of ownership in Kenya and Burkina Faso, that there should be more concern with ownership at both the macro and micro levels in sub-Saharan Africa. What one finds when doing so is that different actors conceptualize ownership based on their positions and preferences in the development realm. More importantly, by focusing on both state and nonstate actors and their interactions with ownership as a paradigm, the restrictive scientific capitalism discourse becomes all the more salient because it sets strict parameters around the roles and responsibilities that actors in Burkina Faso and Kenya can assume if they are to "own" their development.

It matters how and why local actors engage with ownership. This should be a given. However, with respect to much of the development literature on Africa, it is not evident that local actors also matter as important sites for exploring how "best practices" more importantly highlight the ways in which networks of power are activated and deactivated in the world of development. Scholars like Escobar (1995), Esteva (1992), Suárez-Krabbe (2015), Buffardi (2013), Ewig (2011) have explored this perspective in Latin American countries. However, in much of the Africanist scholarship on development, local actors are either pawns with no development objectives of their own or so submersed in their cultural commitments that they become impediments to development. Ownership is a unique entry point into this discussion because it has come to dictate the language, practice, and modalities for progress. Within a given country committed to the paradigm, ownership operates at all levels, the micro, meso, and macro or the community, district, and state levels, because, as Clark noted, it demands broad stakeholder engagement (Clark 2016). Examining stakeholder interactions with ownership in the health sectors of Burkina Faso and Kenya exposes this dynamic. If we widen the analysis beyond institutions to include discourse, then we see that there have been more changes in the local contexts than dominant literature accounts for.

Looking at the discursive practices tied to ownership across local stakeholders in Burkina Faso and Kenya sheds light on the incongruent renderings of ownership that may operate both horizontally and vertically in different African countries. Different stakeholders attach different expectations to the various renderings of ownership, which obfuscates international attempts to measure ownership without understanding local contexts. What informs the different conceptualizations and its consequence for attempting to apply a standard measure of ownership is missing from the literature on ownership. I argue that the varied renderings of ownership in Africa are informed by a type of historical institutionalism whereby the country's initial engagement with structural adjustments acts as a critical juncture for the contemporary interactions with the ownership paradigm (Thelen 1999; Sanders 2008; Fioretos, Falleti, and Sheingate 2016; Lichbach and Zuckerman 2009). In

Burkina Faso, Thomas Sankara's leadership between 1983 and 1987 was grounded in a rejection of both structural adjustments and political aid. In advocating for a model of self-reliant development, the Sankara model was inculcating Burkinabe with a sense of ownership predicated on collective responsibility for progress and resistance to neoimperialism from the West. Alternatively, under Daniel Arap Moi, Kenya was the first African country to accept structural adjustments and, today, it continues to promote a rendering of ownership close to that produced under the dominant ownership paradigm. More importantly, these cases show how the dominant version of ownership may ultimately be reproducing forms of underdevelopment by privileging scientific capitalism as the preeminent strategy for achieving a particular form of development. These findings point to the need to move beyond ownership by decolonizing the discourses associated with it.

The importance of discourse and ideas

Arturo Escobar (1995) explains that development discourse is implemented through practice. Throughout this book, I identify and analyze key discourses that animate and motivate the ownership paradigm, which entails exploring how Burkinabe and Kenyan actors are putting these discourses into practice. One example of such a discourse is that, with ownership, governments are in the driver's seat. The language refers to the ostensible changing relationships around aid so that aid-receiving governments are leading their development and all other stakeholders follow and support. Both Kenyan and Burkinabe stakeholders mobilized this specific language to demonstrate their commitments to owning their development processes.

Capacity building and technical expertise are other discourses operating in the ownership paradigm. By explicitly delineating the roles and expectations for donors working to ameliorate prospects for ownership in aid-receiving countries, capacity building and technical expertise intimate the role of governments and civil society as well. Donors, as builders of capacity, and technical experts align with the World Bank's repositioning of itself as a knowledge-bank, from which African countries can withdraw sound, data-driven, expertise to inform their development decisions (Hill 2002). Further, according to the paradigm, the knowledge that the Bank and other donors harbor should be used to build state-level capacity. UNDP defines capacity building as "the process through which individuals, organizations and societies obtain, strengthen and maintain the capabilities to set and achieve their own development objectives over time" (UNDP 2009). The Paris Declaration commits developing countries to integrate specific capacity strengthening objectives in national development strategies and pursue their implementation through country-led capacity development strategies where needed. The Paris Declaration also commits donors to align their analytic and financial support with partners' capacity development objectives and strategies, make effective use of existing capacities, and harmonize support for capacity development accordingly (OECD 2011, 27). The Accra Agenda for Action (AAA) concretized the focus on capacity building and reinforced previous calls for ownership.

Throughout my time in Burkina Faso and Kenya, the dearth of capacity in African countries, combined with the necessity for donors to bring their expertise as a salient discussion and practice were pervasive tropes across the three stakeholder groups: Government, donors, and civil society organizations (CSOs). While what exactly was meant by capacity and expertise was never clear, the sentiment revolved around the assumption that the Burkinabe and Kenyan governments lacked the tools or knowledge needed to execute development without donors, who supplied the necessary tools and knowledge or expertise to bring forth development. Where Burkinabe and Kenyans were knowledgeable, as some of my informants pointed out, it was about local contexts. The local stakeholders had understandings of their local contexts that would generate important information for donors in their more universal theories. In other words, the capacity building and technical expertise discourse reproduces the notion that Burkinabe and Kenyan actors could only produce provincial knowledge, while donors brought more high-minded and universal knowledge to bear on development problems.

Ideational elements

The traditional perspectives on ownership perpetuate two absolute and incomplete pictures of donor-recipient relations. Either donors have all of the control over policy by using their money as a carrot and stick method to get governments to do what they want (Alemazung 2010), or they are beholden to the policy preferences of recipient governments because they don't have any real enforcement mechanisms and their threats lack credibility (Honig and Gulrajani 2018; Van de Walle and Ndulo 2014). More recently, scholars have tried to put forth a more nuanced view that shows some level of collaboration around modalities for aid delivery, i.e. budget support (Swedlund 2017; Yanguas 2018). While all these perspectives may hold true at the same time, they all miss a very important dimension of the power struggles that underlie the aid framework for many African countries, and that is the ideational level.

Mkandawire aptly notes: "It is probably in this role as an ideational entrepreneur that the international financial institutions (IFIs) have had the most impact on the spread of economic ideas" (2014, 182). He demonstrates how the World Bank and the U.S. government have paid for the training of a considerable number of African economists over the last five decades or so. Their training, however, does not involve economic theory, which would allow the economists to choose from a mélange of different economic theories to fit their national contexts. Instead, the World Bank trains African economists to apply the economic model of the day (Mkandawire 2014). The role of economists in general policymaking has grown across African countries such that, by 2005, thirty-five percent of African leaders were educated in economics or some related field (Mkandawaire 2014, 173). Still, very few scholars have interrogated the influence that ideas and knowledge have on development policy formulation and implementation in Africa, except in the realm of epistemic communities.

Epistemic communities are collective groups of experts or scholars who seek to influence policy by changing the interests of decision-makers in a given realm with a particular type of knowledge that validates their intervention (Haas 1992, 2; Dunlop 2009; Marier 2008; Haas 1989, 398). Scholars demonstrate the ways in which these communities could influence inter-state cooperation by framing policy issues in such a way that states see the need for policy coordination. By leveraging uncertainty, interpretation, and institutionalization, epistemic communities could promote new patterns of behavior at the state level that translate into different policy trajectories.

Uncertainty is key to legitimizing the contributions and presence of an epistemic community in the policy-making arena. The uncertainty that comes with moments of crisis creates a situation in which policy-makers and politicians, by themselves, are unsure of which strategy is best – the assumption being that states seek to reduce uncertainty (Radaelli 1995; Adler and Haas 1992). Desiring to reduce uncertainty means that in moments of crisis, policy-makers are willing to concede power to an epistemic community based on the ability of members of that community to offer consensual knowledge. Consensual knowledge, in turn, is a form of power that insulates the epistemic community's authority over policy-making from outside criticism on the grounds that government officials and those outside the community do not have the epistemic or professional training to challenge the advice (Haas 1989, 398). Uncertainty legitimizes the consensual knowledge coming from the epistemic community, or as Haas states, "In the face of uncertainty, and more so in the wake of a shock or crisis, many of the conditions facilitating a focus on power are absent" (1992, 14). In other words, politicians are so preoccupied with the crisis that they are willing to cede power to the epistemic community in order to address it.

Interpretation is central to the maintenance of an epistemic community because the community, essentially, offers politicians and policy-makers the interpretive lens through which they will view a problem. That there is room for interpreting a crisis allows competing epistemic communities to influence government (Cross 2013; Ewig 2011). To be sure, not only does "the group responsible for articulating the dimensions of reality [have] great social and political influence," it also establishes a space wherein alternative knowledge becomes subjugated (Haas 1992, 14; Foucault 1980). Thus, institutionalization becomes essential for ensuring the community's continued influence over policymaking, with little competition from alternative knowledge sources. Haas (1992) argues that epistemic communities can institutionalize their influence by acquiring bureaucratic power within the national government and at the international level. He states,

> Epistemic communities can insinuate their views and influence national governments and international organizations by occupying niches in advisory and regulatory bodies. This suggests that the application of consensual knowledge to policymaking depends on the ability of the groups transmitting this knowledge to gain and exercise bureaucratic power.
>
> (1992, 30)

Ultimately, epistemic communities, in order to be influential, require some level of permanence within the decision-making apparatus.

Over time, scholars have both reworked and criticized the epistemic communities approach (Toke 1999; Adler 2008).[1] For the purposes of this book, the most salient criticisms and amendments come from Krebs (2001) and Cross (2013). Krebs (2001) proposes that epistemic communities may be composed of scientists whose motivations are not objective and altruistic but, rather, the product of their national backgrounds and strategic interests. This amendment allows for the incorporation of donors into the epistemic community frame. Cross (2013) argues that the definition of epistemic community should include non-academic actors as potential members and non-state actors as potential targets. This means that the binding factor among members of such communities is no longer just scientific knowledge but also professionalism and professional interests. Donors as an epistemic community can (and do) attempt to influence civil society interests as well as government interests.

I explore how through a commitment to ownership of development Kenyan and Burkinabe development actors maintain an epistemic community of Western donors, making a focus on ideas crucial for understanding ownership. There is a long tradition of critical reflection on the implications of the episteme on notions of social, political, and economic progress in the global South (Serra and Stiglitz 2008; Mbembé 2001; Keita 2011; Guardiola-Rivera 2010). The push for ownership that the epistemic community of donors has made since 2005 and subsequent policy changes illustrate the impact that this community of development professionals has in sustaining particular development paradigms. It also demonstrates how ownership thus becomes a necessary mechanism for consolidating the community's influence in domestic policy-making. Few scholars have made the link between epistemic communities and international development, and even fewer have examined the concept as it plays out in the global South, or Africa specifically (Ahu Sandal 2011; Cohendet et al. 2014; Hennemann, Rybski, and Liefner 2012; Youde 2007). Much of the epistemic communities literature relies heavily on Europe as the source of empirical case studies (Adler 2008; Marier 2008; Faleg 2012; Galbreath and McEvoy 2013; Dunlop 2009). Where proponents of the epistemic communities approach have applied this theoretical program to development, it has been uncritical of the "knowledge" that Western donors, as the dominant community, contribute to policymaking. One such example comes from Peter Haas (Haas 2015), who views epistemic communities as valuable actors in carrying out the Millennium Development Goals (MDGs) and global governance programs that lead to sustainable development. In using this lens to explore development in the global South, the heavy influence that donors have had over policy selection in postcolonial African states and societies begins to require critical reflection. Epistemic communities as a theoretical concept help explain donors' continued role in Africa under the pretense of development in crisis. It also helps explain how donors have become permanent fixtures in many African countries.

The World Bank's purported shift towards being a "knowledge bank" and no longer just pecuniary contributes to the need to re-examine ownership and donors for two reasons. First, suggesting that the Bank is just now becoming a source of knowledge willfully neglects the epistemic aid that motivated and legitimized the proliferation of structural adjustment policies in the 1980s and 1990s. Second, it simultaneously exposes the Bank and others proposing epistemic aid to scrutinization of the purported neutrality of their knowledge.

What the Kenyan case specifically contributes is an account of the ways in which epistemic communities produce discourses or behaviors and practices that demonstrate membership in the community. For example, there is a lexis or jargon associated with any community (Escobar 1995; Swales 2011). Entrance into an epistemic community requires that one demonstrate a mastery of the jargon, practices, and discourses internal to the community. In the Kenyan case, the government adopted the various grammars tied to ownership in ways that would demonstrate knowledge of and commitment to development, but donors did not consider the Kenyan government a part of their epistemic community.

Ownership in the literature

Scholars are divided on how feasible and realistic ownership is in African contexts. Buiter (2007), for example, argues that ownership is another empty development buzzword. Others argue that ownership is primarily an imposition of ideas from donors (Cheru 2006; Shiverenje 2005; Mkandawire 2014; Ferguson 2006). For example, Thandika Mkandawire explains that

> [t]o solve the principal-agent problems that bedeviled conditionality, it was argued that "ownership" of policymaking must be transferred to nationals. This was to be achieved in two ways. One way was to maintain the charade whereby key position papers such as those for meetings of the Paris Club, which supposedly reflected government opinion, were ghost-written by donors who then turned around and praised the recipients for their thoughtful propositions.
>
> (Mkandawire 2014, 184)

After interrogating ownership in Mali and Ghana, Brown (2017) found that both governments had adopted aspects of ownership because they had both elaborated national development plans that were not imposed on them by donors. However, based on the measurements for ownership outlined by the OECD, neither country is fully engaged in that process because there is no prioritization of development plans, and neither country has fully implemented its plans. Brolin (2017) examines the power relations surrounding ownership in Mozambique. Looking specifically at Swedish budget support, she finds that the Swedish government adopts the language of results-based development and ownership in its engagement with the Mozambican government; however, the Swedish government continues to demand reports on the Mozambican government's activities and processes towards specific goals in order to hold the government accountable. Brolin argues that the Swedish government's focus on process and accountability conflicts with the language of results-based development and impedes ownership in Mozambique.

The scholarly discussions of ownership give far too much importance to donor-government relations for the same reason that ownership became a prominent topic in the early 2000s in the first place: The need to address principal-agent problems surrounding conditionalities. Donor agencies are the principals and African states are the agents, and their relationship is often riddled with mistrust. Information between the two parties can be asymmetrical in the sense that donors are unsure of whether governments will properly execute and remain committed to policies or programs. Conditionalities were designed as an earlier solution to this problem, but these have a poor track record for bringing about sustainable progress (Chikulo 1997; Gould 2005). Khan and Sharma theorize ownership as

> a situation in which the policy content of the program is similar to what the country itself would have chosen in the absence of IMF involvement. . . . In such a situation, the country "owns" the program in the sense that it is committed to the spirit of the program, rather than just to comply with its letter.
>
> (2001, 13–14)

Donors have turned to ownership as an alternative, with advocates suggesting that a principal-agent view of ownership coalesces the demands of borrowers and lenders, harmonizing their incentives in ways that make it more likely that governments will remain committed to development policies.

In theory, country ownership could address a number of complications that often arise with principals and agents in the aid realm, the most pressing and costly of which are monitoring and evaluation (Holvoet and Renard 2007). With ownership, donor agencies can be more certain that African governments are using funds for the purposes for which they were intended, enabling donors to reduce money spent, as with conditionalities, on monitoring. Resolving fundamental problems of traditional donor-recipient relationships while replacing tedious conditionalities would presumably increase aid's effectiveness (Khan and Sharma 2001; Pender 2001). The impediment to ownership here is the neopatrimonial African state, leading scholars to question the feasibility of ownership in Africa due to a dearth of capacity and governance (Kasekende 2006). For example, David Booth opines that, with respect to ownership,

> The concept makes the diplomatic assumption that recipient countries are already led by people for whom national development is a central objective. I would argue that this is not an assumption that may be made generally or without heavy qualification, at least in the region that mostly concerns me, sub-Saharan Africa.
>
> (Booth 2011, 540)

Not everyone exploring ownership in Africa from the donor-government perspective has employed the principal-agent framework. For example, Carlsson, Somolekae, and van de Walle (1997) sought to measure ownership in Africa by examining donor-government relations, looking specifically at the degree to which donor procedures and needs drove the direction of foreign aid and the impact of donor conditionalities on development projects and programs. For Carlsson, Somolekae, and van de Walle (1997), the origin and impetus for development policies factored heavily into whether or not the country truly owned its development. When assessing how much control the Ghanaian government exercises over development, for instance, they observed that "about 35 percent of [policy] proposals for bilateral projects are prepared with significant donor input, while project design is either completely in the hands of donors or partially controlled by the donor" (1997, 95). Across their various African cases, the authors found very limited evidence of country ownership.

For contributors to Whitfield (2009), ownership is also a matter of government control over the design and implementation of development policy. They ground their conceptualization of ownership in John Stuart Mill's foundational notion of sovereignty. For Mill, "non-intervention provided a protected space for societies to struggle for and amongst themselves" (Whitfield 2009, 7). Sovereignty as a political space within which states are free to arrange their domestic affairs without undue pressure or unwanted involvement from foreign actors sets a much higher threshold for ownership than the existing framework for aid-dependent countries. When one undergirds ownership in pursuit of national sovereignty, the outcome is ownership as collective local command of development strategies. There is limited ownership in Africa by this standard. As Whitfield argues,

> the willingness of powerful states to accept a plurality of domestic political arrangements and developmental visions has weakened, and the "right" to sovereignty for weaker states has gradually been made conditional upon meeting responsibilities imposed by the international community.
>
> (2009, 8)

Analyzing ownership in Africa as a matter of sovereignty or state control over policy direction and implementation means that donors are the ones who impede the possibility of ownership in Africa, not the other way around.[2]

All these analyses reinforce ownership as a problem between donors and governments,[3] but this is merely one aspect of the paradigm. As I stated previously, civil society's contributions to country-level ownership were a significant part of the third OECD High Level forum in Accra, Ghana. Despite the irony of civil society's importance for ownership being championed in Ghana, the role of African civil societies in carrying out ownership has been virtually nonexistent.

It may be that few scholars have considered the ways in which African civil societies negotiate and implement ownership because of the putative assumptions about civil societies in Africa writ large. First, as an analytical category, civil society does not neatly reconcile with African realities, illustrating the limited utility of the concept for comparison across spatial, temporal, and cultural contexts (Comaroff and Comaroff 1999). Second, even when donors and scholars force the concept onto existing contexts in postcolonial Africa, one still finds a dearth of possibility for an autonomous civil society (Mbembé 2001; Mamdani 1996; Amutabi 2013). This ends up being the case in both Kenya and Burkina Faso, where most local associations and nongovernmental organizations, which make of the bulk of CSOs, exist because of donor and government funding. Donors in both countries also use CSOs to circumvent governments and make local interventions when donors are frustrated with government implementation. Under the ownership paradigm, CSOs are supposed to represent a space wherein nongovernmental and nonmarket actors can speak on behalf of the general population with respect to broad stakeholder engagement. CSOs are also expected to aid donors in holding government accountable for implementing policies. In this way, they are especially important for exploring ownership. Perhaps more importantly, including a focus on civil society actors in Burkina Faso and Kenya also highlights the need to abandon assumptions that power dynamics in the aid architecture can only be understood between the donors and the state, because CSOs are integral to the execution and maintenance of national development. Unpacking and analyzing the ways in which civil society organizations navigate donors and the state by adopting or rejecting development discourses should be standard in any analysis of development in Africa.

Methods

I use health as the development sector to situate this study and seventy-five original, semi-structured interviews and participant observations from Burkina Faso and Kenya to understand the matrix of actions and practices for negotiating ownership. I conducted fieldwork for a total of four months: Two months in Kenya (one month in June 2013 and five weeks from December 2015 through January 2016) and two months in Burkina Faso (June through August 2015). I spoke with top-ranking government officials and policymakers in the Ministries of Health (MoH) and Finance.[4] In Kenya, I interviewed government officials in the External Resource Department (ERD), located in the National Treasury. In Burkina Faso, I interviewed policy makers in la Direction Générale de l'Economie et de la Planification (DGEP or General Directorate for the Economy and Planning). The government officials in the ERD and DGEP were able to speak to their respective country's economic and national development strategies and the degree to which donors were involved in elaborating these strategies. These departments and the MoH represent the government stakeholder under the ownership paradigm.

I also interviewed and observed donors. In Burkina Faso, I spoke with representatives from the U.S. Agency for International Development (USAID), the U.S. Peace Corps, the United Nations Population Fund (UNFPA), and the World Bank. In Kenya, I interviewed representatives from the Japanese International Cooperation Agency (JICA), the European Union, the Danish International Development Agency (DANIDA), and the World Bank. Admittedly, there is considerable variation across donor organizations and their aid practices (Easterly and Williamson 2011; Easterly and Pfutze 2008).[5] Despite this divergence, all of the donors that I interviewed had, at the very least, signed on to the Paris Declaration and have at one point or another endorsed the need for ownership. I supplement these interviews with analysis of donor policies from donor-funded global initiatives, such as the International Conference on Population Development (ICPD), the Millennium Development Goals (MDGs), and the Sustainable Development Goals (SDGs), to understand international donors' discourse and policies towards health.

Discourse is the central analytical category in this book. As such, I apply critical discourse analysis to the interviews, participant observations, and policy documents from both cases. Critical discourse analysis gives primacy to the semiotic facets of power and change within economic, political, and/or social structures (Carant 2017; Weiss and Wodak 2007; Fairclough 2013; Vavrus and Seghers 2010). Focusing on the semiotics of ownership in these two health systems clarifies the dialectical relationship between discursive events, i.e. local actors' manipulation of the paradigm and the institutions, and the social structures that frame their manipulations, as well as how each of these – both the events and the contexts – are intersubjective (Fairclough 2013; Fairclough, Wodak, and Mulderrig 2003), the end goal being to expose the consequences of this dialectical relationship on power relations in development practices particular to Kenya and Burkina Faso.

Case selection

Because the ownership paradigm heavily implicates civil society in the development process, I interviewed representatives from civil society organizations such as NGOs and community-based organizations (CBOs). I observed meetings between representatives from the local health associations of Tenkodogo (Burkina Faso) and their funding NGO regarding local efforts to implement the national health sector strategy. I participated in the Economic Cooperation of West African States' (ECOWAS) Good Practices

Forum in Health from July 29–31, 2015. The Forum's theme was "Ending Preventable Mother and Child Deaths in West Africa – What Works in Reproductive Health and Family Planning." Member states from West Africa, donors, including USAID and the World Bank, and civil society associations from across West Africa presented research on maternal and child health, understood largely as the need to increase the adoption of family planning methods. In Kenya and Burkina Faso, the health sector continues to receive government funding; however, service delivery occurs predominantly through NGOs. Examining the sphere of civil society demonstrates how ownership percolates through to the everyday activities of Kenyans and Burkinabe and does not stay at the level of abstract, technical development jargon.

I chose Kenya and Burkina Faso as the case studies to understand how agents are interpreting, creating, and navigating the ownership discourse on the ground because of their distinct histories with donors, their economic positions within their respective sub-regions of Africa, and for variation across colonial histories and geography. Kenya, a strong political player in the East Africa region, is notorious for its "hot and cold" relationship with donors; it represents a case in which government officials and members of civil society attempt to use ownership as a form of leverage vis-à-vis donor preferences. Geographically, Kenya straddles the equator and has access to ports along its Eastern coast.[6] Kenya has also been amenable to market-based approaches to development since independence. Chapters three and four explore the long-term ramifications of Kenya's commitment to market-based strategies on local approaches to ownership. Burkina Faso has remained one of the more politically stable countries in West Africa, despite being one of the poorest by GDP standards.[7] The country is also land-locked and situated in the far southern Sahara and across the Sahel. Unlike Kenya, Burkina Faso experienced a revolutionary period of anti-imperialism and anti-market-driven development from 1983 until 1987. In Chapter four, I argue that this brief revolutionary period has had direct implications for Burkinabe stakeholders and their interpretations of ownership. In both countries, I use health as a sectoral backdrop for analyzing development policies.

Although the ownership paradigm encompasses all development sectors, education, agriculture, technology, and infrastructure, *inter alia*, I found health to be the sector that has wholly adopted the paradigm and all of its accompanying tools and discourses.[8] In 2015, an unprecedented Ebola outbreak in Sierra Leone, Liberia, and Guinea brought global health to the forefront of many domestic-level policy discussions (Davies and Bennett 2016). The epidemic lasted for roughly two years, from 2014 until 2016. In 2018, another Ebola outbreak started in the Democratic Republic of Congo, in the Kivu region – a region already marred by unyielding conflict. These events called into question the health infrastructure in these and other African countries. They also point to a need to assess the strategies and policies that African countries are adopting to strengthen their health systems. Scholars have argued, as I do here, that globally, as well as in much of Africa, health policies and strategies continue to reflect neoliberal commitments, where states relinquish control over service delivery in healthcare to the private sector and non-state entities (Ayo 2012; Rowden 2009; Kenny 2015; Ravindran 2014). However, the underlying assumption is *not* that some African governments and civil society organizations do not wholly favor the neoliberal healthcare strategy but, rather, that these policies are imposed on African states by donors. I demonstrate how, by feeling as though they "own" these policies, some Burkinabe and Kenyan stakeholders promote these institutions as the best means for developing their health sectors. The health sector proved more generative a space for exploring ownership in both countries because it is assumed to be a value-neutral and apolitical development domain.

Understanding the ways in which hegemony of knowledge production plays out in the health sector is crucial because of what health represents to development practitioners: An objective space concerned only with the saving of lives through modern means (Davies and Bennett 2016). Modern medicine, rife with a history of racism and sexism, is not a value-neutral space; modern medicine continuously reproduces and maintains hierarchies of power (Kenny 2015; Ayo 2012; Rowden 2009; Ravindran 2014; Ewig 2011). Health in Africa has been and remains a site of power and privilege mediated through knowledge and material production (Chapman 2016; Waitzkin 2015). Exploring how the ownership paradigm constructs this matrix and how Kenyans and Burkinabe navigate (and at times reproduce) the matrix revealed differences between both countries and their health sectors. My findings for Burkina Faso detail how community-based organizations negotiate owning development around family planning policy and programming. In Kenya, I focus on how ownership negotiation unfolds at the state level between donors and government officials with respect to health sector strategies writ large. The difference in levels of analysis is less a product of intentional focus and more the result of an inductive approach to studying ownership in the health sectors of both countries.

Overemphasis on PEA

Political economy analysis (PEA) has become the go-to analytical frame for development scholars and practitioners looking at ownership. Development scholars use PEA to take factors like history, politics, and geography into account when attempting to solve a country-specific development problem. PEA practitioners acknowledge that politics play a role in development and so, too, do local contexts. These factors are taken as structural constraints on stakeholder options. Institutions also figure into the analysis as key for understanding the limits of change in a given country.

Proponents of the PEA framework also depend on the principle of ownership for effective implementation and outcomes, which leads to inconsistencies in its application. Fisher and Marquette observe that PEA

> reflects a wider crisis in contemporary development policy-making (at least among OECD-DAC [Development Assistance Committee] donors) whereby enthusiasm for ownership and partnership-led approaches rub up against the difficulties of working in states where authorities remain uncommitted to core Western donor agendas such as poverty reduction and good governance, and where increasing (re)integration of development agencies into foreign ministries often brings to the fore concerns with ensuring aid outcomes are aligned with donors' national interests.
>
> (2016, 116)

The authors also argue that looking at ownership through PEA demonstrates clear limitations for donors on the ground because PEA is still donor-centric, not transparent, and does not genuinely incorporate aid-recipient stakeholders, highlighting the limitations of putting ownership into practice (Fisher and Marquette 2016).

One of the major limitations of PEA is that it frames donors as distant observers when, in fact, many donor organizations have long been embedded agents in designing institutions and structures in many African countries. A PEA conducted by donors is almost the antithesis of the ownership model. If there were a genuine desire to allow states to take the lead and for donors to give up control, then donors should easily defer to local stakeholders who are more likely to know the webs of power and various social, political, and economic institutions that influence their development actions. If that were the case, donors would trust these actors enough to simply fund their development requests, confident that local stakeholders have the information necessary to make needs assessments themselves. But instead, we see donors continuing to use frameworks like PEA to figure out the best way to change local environments and increase the effectiveness of the donors' financial and epistemic commitments.

More importantly, scholars who use the PEA framework to explore ownership cannot account for the role of ideas and knowledge-making internal to the paradigm and the process towards ownership. To the extent that ideas become an essential focus, it is with respect to their ability to change local actors' preferences and behaviors. Or, donors give lip-service to local knowledge as important when attempting an intervention at the local level.[9] The PEA framework and others like it are incomplete in that they suppose a unidirectional flow of ideas and information, as well as the assumption that change must be purposeful and orchestrated. Instead, what I submit here is that through engagement with the ownership paradigm, local actors in Burkina Faso and Kenya are not only changing their actions in ways that conform with the dictates of ownership, but also bending and navigating aspects of the paradigm to serve their aims. These micro-shifts are much more evident when one focuses on the discursive aspects of ownership.

The utility of ownership is in its ostensible universal application across all aid-dependent cases, especially those in Africa (World Bank 2000; OECD 2011; Boughton 2003). If this were so, I should be able to select at random any country in Africa that is party to the ownership paradigm and see that country setting its own agendas and donors harmonizing and aligning with local priorities and agendas. Throughout this book, I generalize more so the problems inherent in the paradigm that, for a variety of reasons, do not allow for genuine country-specific development. I do not want to generalize the experiences that are particular to Burkina Faso and Kenya across the continent.

Conclusion

If discourse refers to the language and practices that (re)produce relations of power between actors, then any attempt to assess whether or not the owner-ship paradigm has created a shift in traditional power dynamics between donors and local development actors cannot exclude discourse from the analysis. This is not to say that institutions and other factors are not useful, but that they do not provide a complete picture. What discourse is intended to reflect is a new way of doing development that ostensibly incorporates the types of ownership that African leaders and communities have demanded since colonialism ended formally. It implies that donors have handed over the steering wheel to African governments and that, with increased owner-ship, power shifts are underway.

Until now, scholars and development practitioners have demanded more ownership for African countries, whether it meant more commitment from African governments to donor policies or African governments' having more control over the policy process. In both instances, advocates of owner-ship entreat African governments to adopt the tools, language, and practices associated with the version of ownership coming from the OECD's high-level fora since 2003, which have now become paradigmatic. Scholars and development practitioners, in their calls for more ownership in Africa, have also fixed their gazes on institution-building and the interactions between African states and donors. Shifting the focus to incorporate civil society actors, local interpretations, and discourse initiates a more complete picture of ownership.

Refocusing the lens to incorporate local stakeholder interpretations and discourse exposes how the ownership paradigm can be limiting or emancipatory for Burkinabe and Kenyan stakeholders pursuing development. The paradigm is not altogether emancipatory as many believe. Its limitations are embedded in the ideas and discourses that motivate the call for ownership. The larger discourse is that of scientific capitalism: Burkina Faso and Kenya own development to the extent that they both are implementing health policies that transform each country into modern capitalist countries. But development practitioners and scholars must first start the process of decolonizing ownership before it can truly lead to country-specific and country-led development.

Notes

1 Anthony Zito (2001) argues that epistemic communities should consider that national institutions are not necessarily open to receiving new ideas; Emanuel Adler (2008) proposes that epistemic communities function along similar lines as "communities of practice." Thus, the focus is on the particular actions associated with the community's advice and not the specific "knowledge" *per se.*

2 Swedlund (2017) argues that African governments and donors are both guilty of hampering the benefits of aid by failing to meet their respective commitments. She argues that donors cannot evade negotiating with aid-receiving governments because the governments must consent to donors working within their borders; donors need governments to execute programs and implement projects, and to enforce the policies attached to the aid. Her analysis of donor-government relations in aid-dependent Africa intimates that there is an equal partnership between donors and recipients, which contradicts the gestalt of empirical analyses on ownership.

3 More recently, scholars have examined ownership between donors and supranational organizations in Africa. For example, Söderbaum (2017) examines the application of ownership in African regional organizations. Looking specifically at aid from the Swedish government, he finds that the Swedish government tends to overemphasize capacity building in the Secretariats but not with government officials in the aid-receiving countries.

4 In Kenya, the Ministry of Finance is now the National Treasury, and in Burkina Faso, the official title is the Ministry of Finance and Economics (MOFE).

5 Some of the divergent practices among donors came out in my interviews with donors. Consistently, multilateral donors, and government officials in Burkina Faso and Kenya listed USAID as being one of the worst organizations to work with in terms of adhering to the government's development strategies, not using country systems, and circumventing government to deliver aid. The field

of development economics is also not so monolithic. The economics discourse that I discuss throughout this book dominates development economics and has become institutionalized in international development practices.

6 I take geography into account with case selection because of its importance as a key explanatory variable for development (Sachs 2006; Acemoglu, Johnson, and Robinson 2000). Countries with ports and moderate climates favorable to European habitation, like Kenya, are expected to have institutions that are more amenable to liberal development. Alternatively, countries like Burkina Faso, which is land-locked, hot, and not favorable to European habitation, should have more extractive institutions.

7 In the fall of 2014, Burkina Faso experienced a coup d'état that ousted President Blaise Comparé, who had been in power for close to thirty years.

8 I began this project looking at the education sector in Kenya and found it difficult for two reasons. One, the Kenyan government had recently experienced a high-profile case of corruption with its SWAp for education, the Kenyan Education Sector Support Program (KESSP), where millions of Kenyan shillings (Ksh) in donor funding for education went missing. It was extremely difficult to ask questions about ownership of education policy in the shadow of such a scandal. Two, the education system was particularly rife with overt political tensions. Teachers were constantly on strike over lack of pay and the dearth of resources. CSO engagement in the education sector was also not as prominent as it was in the health sector.

9 Referencing a quote from the World Bank, that "Indigenous knowledge provides the basis for problem-solving strategies for local communities, especially the poor and the formerly marginalized. It represents an important component of global knowledge on development issues," Mawere notes that in many African countries, development practitioners continue to underutilize indigenous knowledge when elaborating development plans (2014, 27).

References

Acemoglu, Daron, Simon Johnson, and James A. Robinson. 2000. "The Colonial Origins of Comparative Development: An Empirical Investigation." NBER Working Paper No. 7771. doi: 10.3386/w7771.

Adler, Emanuel. 2008. "The Spread of Security Communities: Communities of Practice, Self-Restraint, and NATO's Post-Cold War Transformation." *European Journal of International Relations* 14 (2): 195–230.

Adler, Emanuel, and Peter M. Haas. 1992. "Conclusion: Epistemic Communities, World Order, and the Creation of a Reflective Research Program." *International Organization* 46 (1): 367–90.

Ahu Sandal, Nukhet. 2011. "Religious Actors as Epistemic Communities in Conflict Transformation: The Cases of South Africa and Northern Ireland." *Review of International Studies* 37 (3): 929–49.

Alemazung, Joy Asongazoh. 2010. "Post-Colonial Colonialism: An Analysis of International Factors and Actors Marring African Socio-Economic and Political Development." *The Journal of Pan African Studies* 3 (10): 62–84.

Amutabi, Maurice N. 2013. *The NGO Factor in Africa: The Case of Arrested Development in Kenya.* New York: Routledge.

Ayo, Nike. 2012. "Understanding Health Promotion in a Neoliberal Climate and the Making of Health Conscious Citizens." *Critical Public Health* 22 (1): 99–105.

Booth, David. 2011. "Aid, Institutions and Governance: What Have We Learned?" *Development Policy Review* 29 (s1): s5–s26.

Boughton, James M. 2003. "Who's in Charge? Ownership and Conditionality in IMF-Supported Programs." International Monetary Fund Working Paper. www. imf.org/en/Publications/WP/Issues/2016/12/30/Who-s-in-Charge-Ownership-and-Conditionality-in-IMF-Supported-Programs-16796.

Brolin, Therese. 2017. "Ownership and Results in Swedish General Budget Support to Mozambique." *Forum for Development Studies* 44 (3): 377–99.

Brown, Stephen. 2017. "Foreign Aid and National Ownership in Mali and Ghana." *Forum for Development Studies* 44 (3): 335–56.

Buffardi, Anne L. 2013. "Configuring 'Country Ownership': Patterns of Donor-Recipient Relations." *Development in Practice* 23 (8): 977–90.

Buiter, Willem. 2007. "Country Ownership, A Term Whose Time Has Gone." *Development in Practice* 17 (4–5): 647–52.

Carant, Jane Briant. 2017. "Unheard Voices: A Critical Discourse Analysis of the Millennium Development Goals' Evolution into the Sustainable Development Goals." *Third World Quarterly* 38 (1): 16–41.

Carlsson, Jerker, Gloria Somolekae, and Nicolas van de Walle, eds. 1997. *Foreign Aid in Africa: Learning from Country Experiences.* New Brunswick: Transaction Publishers.

Chapman, Audrey R. 2016. *Human Rights, Global Health, and Neoliberal Policies.* Cambridge: Cambridge University Press.

Cheru, Fantu. 2006. "Building and Supporting PRSPs in Africa: What Has Worked Well So Far? What Needs Changing?" *Third World Quarterly* 27 (2): 355–76.

Clark, Helen. 2016. "Helen Clark: Statement on Africa and the 2030 Sustainable Development Agenda: Mobilizing the Means of Implementation at High-Level Side Event on the Margins of the 2016 UN High Level Political Forum." United Nations Development Programme. July 18, 2016. www.undp.org/content/undp/en/home/presscenter/speeches/2016/07/18/helen-clark-statement-on-africa-and-the-2030-sustainable-development-agenda-mobilizing-the-means-of-implementation-at-high-level-side-event-on-the-margins-of-the-2016-un-high-level-political-forum.html.

Cohendet, Patrick; Grandadam, David; Simon, Laurent; Capdevila, Ignasi. 2014. "Epistemic Communities, Localization and the Dynamics of Knowledge Creation." *Journal of Economic Geography* 14 (5): 929–54.

Comaroff, John L., and Jean Comaroff. 1999. *Civil Society and the Political Imagination in Africa: Critical Perspectives.* Chicago: University of Chicago Press.

Cross, Mai'A K. Davis. 2013. "Rethinking Epistemic Communities Twenty Years Later." *Review of International Studies* 39 (1): 137–60.

Davies, Sara E., and Belinda Bennett. 2016. "A Gendered Human Rights Analysis of Ebola and Zika: Locating Gender in Global Health Emergencies." *International Affairs* 92 (5): 1041–60.

Dunlop, Claire A. 2009. "Policy Transfer as Learning: Capturing Variation in What Decision-Makers Learn from Epistemic Communities." *Policy Studies* 30 (3): 289–311.

Theorizing ownership 37

Easterly, William, and Claudia R. Williamson. 2011. "Rhetoric versus Reality: The Best and Worst of Aid Agency Practices." *World Development* 39 (11): 1930–49.

Easterly, William, and Tobias Pfutze. 2008. "Where Does the Money Go? Best and Worst Practices in Foreign Aid." *The Journal of Economic Perspectives* 22 (2): 29–52.

Escobar, Arturo. 1995. *Encountering Development: The Making and Unmaking of the Third World.* Princeton, NJ: Princeton University Press.

Esteva, Gustavo. 1992. "Development." In *The Development Dictionary: A Guide to Knowledge as Power*, edited by Wolfgang Sachs, 6–25. London: Zed Books.

Ewig, Christina. 2011. *Second-Wave Neoliberalism: Gender, Race, and Health Sector Reform in Peru.* University Park, PA: Pennsylvania State Press.

Fairclough, Norman. 2013. "Critical Discourse Analysis and Critical Policy Studies." *Critical Policy Studies* 7 (2): 177–97.

Fairclough, Norman, Ruth Wodak, and Jane Mulderrig. 2003. "Critical Discourse Analysis." In *Discourse Studies: A Multidisciplinary Introduction*, edited by Teun A. van Dijk, 85–109. London: Palgrave Macmillan.

Faleg, Giovanni. 2012. "Between Knowledge and Power: Epistemic Communities and the Emergence of Security Sector Reform in the EU Security Architecture." *European Security* 21 (2): 161–84.

Ferguson, James. 2006. *Global Shadows: Africa in the Neoliberal World Order.* Durham, NC: Duke University Press.

Fioretos, Orfeo, Tulia G. Falleti, and Adam Sheingate. 2016. *The Oxford Handbook of Historical Institutionalism.* Oxford: Oxford University Press.

Fisher, Jonathan, and Heather Marquette. 2016. "'Empowered Patient' or 'Doctor Knows Best'? Political Economy Analysis and Ownership." *Development in Practice* 26 (1): 115–26.

Foucault, Michel. 1980. *Power/Knowledge: Selected Interviews and Other Writings, 1972–1977.* New York: Pantheon.

Galbreath, David J., and Joanne McEvoy. 2013. "How Epistemic Communities Drive International Regimes: The Case of Minority Rights in Europe." *Journal of European Integration* 35 (2): 169–86.

Gould, Jeremy. 2005. *The New Conditionality: The Politics of Poverty Reduction Strategies.* London: Zed books.

Grosfoguel, Ramón. 2007. "The Epistemic Decolonial Turn." *Cultural Studies* 21 (2–3): 211–23.

Guardiola-Rivera, Oscar. 2010. *What If Latin America Ruled the World? How the South Will Take the North into the 22nd Century.* London: Bloomsbury Publishing.

Haas, Peter M. 1989. "Do Regimes Matter? Epistemic Communities and Mediterranean Pollution Control." *International Organization* 43 (3): 377–403.

———. 1992. "Introduction: Epistemic Communities and International Policy Coordination." *International Organization* 46 (1): 1–35.

Haas, Peter M. 2015. *Epistemic Communities, Constructivism, and International Environmental Politics.* London: Routledge.

Hennemann, Stefan, Diego Rybski, and Ingo Liefner. 2012. "The Myth of Global Science Collaboration–Collaboration Patterns in Epistemic Communities." *Journal of Informetrics* 6 (2): 217–25.

Hill, Peter S. 2002. "The Rhetoric of Sector-Wide Approaches for Health Development." *Social Science & Medicine* 54 (11): 1725–37.

Holvoet, N., and Robrecht Renard. 2007. "Monitoring and Evaluation under the PRSP: Solid Rock or Quicksand?" *Evaluation and Program Planning* 30 (1): 66–81.

Honig, Dan, and Nilima Gulrajani. 2018. "Making Good on Donors' Desire to Do Development Differently." *Third World Quarterly* 39 (1): 68–84.

Kasekende, Louis. 2006. "Country Ownership of Policy Reforms and Aid Effectiveness: The Challenge of Enhancing the Policy Space for Developing Countries in Aid Relationships." Statement presented at the Aid as Negotiation: Workshop, Oxford, September 26.

Keita, L. D., ed. 2011. *Philosophy and African Development: Theory and Practice.* Dakar, Senegal: Codesria.

Kenny, Katherine E. 2015. "The Biopolitics of Global Health: Life and Death in Neoliberal Time." *Journal of Sociology* 51 (1): 9–27.

Khan, Mohsin S., and Sunil Sharma. 2001. *IMF Conditionality and Country Ownership of Programs (EPub).* Washington, DC: International Monetary Fund.

Krebs, Ronald. 2001. "The Limits of Alliance: Conflict, Cooperation, and Collective Identity." In *The Real and the Ideal: Essays on International Relations in Honor of Richard H. Ullman*, edited by Richard Henry Ullman, David A. Ochmanek, and Ronald Krebs. Lanham: Rowman & Littlefield.

Lichbach, Mark Irving, and Alan S. Zuckerman, eds. 2009. *Comparative Politics: Rationality, Culture, and Structure.* Cambridge: Cambridge University Press.

Maldonado-Torres, Nelson. 2007. "On the Coloniality of Being." *Cultural Studies* 21 (2–3): 240–70.

Mamdani, Mahmood. 1996. *Citizen and Subject: Contemporary African and the Legacy of Late Colonialism.* Princeton, NJ: Princeton University Press.

Marier, Patrik. 2008. "Empowering Epistemic Communities: Specialised Politicians, Policy Experts and Policy Reform." *West European Politics* 31 (3): 513–33.

Mawere, Munyaradzi. 2014. *Culture, Indigenous Knowledge and Development in Africa: Reviving Interconnections for Sustainable Development.* Bamenda: Langaa RPCIG.

Mbembé, J.-A. 2001. *On the Postcolony.* Berkeley: University of California Press.

Meyer, Stefan, and Nils-Sjard Schulz. 2008. "Ownership with Adjectives, Donor Harmonisation: Between Effectiveness and Democratisation." *Synthesis Report.* www.researchgate.net/publication/237811264_Ownership_with_Adjectives_ Donor_Harmonisation_Between_Effectiveness_and_Democratisation_Synthe sis_Report.

Mignolo, Walter. 2009. "Epistemic Disobedience, Independent Thought and Decolonial Freedom." *Theory, Culture & Society* 26 (7–8): 159–81.

Mkandawire, Thandika. 2014. "The Spread of Economic Doctrines and Policymaking in Postcolonial Africa." *African Studies Review* 57 (01): 171–98.

Ndlovu-Gatsheni, Sabelo J. 2015. "Decoloniality as the Future of Africa." *History Compass* 13 (10): 485–96.

OECD. 2011. *Aid Effectiveness 2005–10: Progress in Implementing the Paris Declaration.* OECD Publishing.

Pender, John. 2001. "From Structural Adjustment to Comprehensive Development Framework: Conditionality Transformed?" *Third World Quarterly* 22 (3): 397–411.

Quan, H. L. T. 2012. *Growth against Democracy: Savage Developmentalism in the Modern World.* Lanham, MD: Lexington Books.

Quijano, Aníbal. 2007. "Coloniality and Modernity/Rationality." *Cultural Studies* 21 (2–3): 168–78.

Radaelli, Claudio M. 1995. "The Role of Knowledge in the Policy Process." *Journal of European Public Policy* 2 (2): 159–83.

Ravindran, TK Sundari. 2014. "Poverty, Food Security and Universal Access to Sexual and Reproductive Health Services: A Call for Cross-Movement Advocacy against Neoliberal Globalisation." *Reproductive Health Matters* 22 (43): 14–27.

Rowden, Rick. 2009. *The Deadly Ideas of Neoliberalism: How the IMF Has Undermined Public Health and the Fight against AIDS.* London: Zed Books.

Sachs, Jeffrey D. 2006. *The End of Poverty: Economic Possibilities for Our Time.* New York: Penguin Press.

Sachs, Wolfgang, ed. 1992. *The Development Dictionary: A Guide to Knowledge as Power.* London and Atlantic Highlands, NJ: St. Martin's Press.

Sanders, Elizabeth. 2008. "Historical Institutionalism." In *The Oxford Handbook of Political Institutions,* edited by R. A. W. Rhodes, Sarah A. Binder, and Bert A. Rockman. Oxford: Oxford University Press.

Serra, Narcís, and Joseph E. Stiglitz. 2008. *The Washington Consensus Reconsidered: Towards a New Global Governance: Towards a New Global Governance.* Oxford: Oxford University Press.

Shiverenje, Hudson. 2005. "What Happened to the PRSP in Kenya? The Role of Politics." *PLA Notes* 51: 27–31.

Söderbaum, Fredrik. 2017. "Swedish Development Cooperation and Ownership of African Regional Organizations." *Forum for Development Studies* 44 (3): 357–75.

Suárez-Krabbe, Julia. 2015. *Race, Rights, and Rebels: Alternatives to Human Rights and Development from the Global South.* London: Rowman & Littlefield International.

Swales, J. 2011. "The Concept of Discourse Community." In *Writing About Writing: A College Reader,* edited by Douglas Downs and Elizabeth Wardle. London: Bedford/St. Martin's.

Swedlund, Haley J. 2017. *The Development Dance: How Donors and Recipients Negotiate the Delivery of Foreign Aid.* Ithaca, NY: Cornell University Press.

Thelen, Kathleen. 1999. "Historical Institutionalism in Comparative Politics." *Annual Review of Political Science* 2 (1): 369–404.

Toke, Dave. 1999. "Epistemic Communities and Environmental Groups." *Politics* 19 (2): 97–102.

UNDP. 2009. "Capacity Development: A UNDP Primer." United Nations Development Programme. www.undp.org/content/undp/en/home/librarypage/capacity-building/capacity-development-a-undp-primer.html.

United States Government. 2012. "U.S. Government Interagency Paper on Country Ownership: Global Health Initiative."

Van de Walle, Nicolas, and Muna Ndulo. 2014. *Problems, Promises, and Paradoxes of Aid: Africa's Experience.* Newcastle upon Tyne: Cambridge Scholars Publishing.

Vavrus, Frances, and Maud Seghers. 2010. "Critical Discourse Analysis in Comparative Education: A Discursive Study of 'Partnership' in Tanzania's Poverty Reduction Policies." *Comparative Education Review* 54 (1): 77–103.

Waitzkin, Howard. 2015. *Medicine and Public Health at the End of Empire.* London and New York: Routledge.

Weiss, Gilbert, and Ruth Wodak, eds. 2007. *Critical Discourse Analysis.* New York: Springer.

Whitfield, Lindsay, ed. 2009. *The Politics of Aid: African Strategies for Dealing with Donors.* New York: Oxford University Press.

World Bank. 2000. *Attacking Poverty.* Edited by S. M. Ravi Kanbur and Nora Lustig. World Development Report, 2000/2001. New York: Published for the World Bank, Oxford University Press.

Yanguas, Pablo. 2018. *Why We Lie about Aid.* London: Zed Books.

Youde, Jeremy R. 2007. *AIDS, South Africa, and the Politics of Knowledge.* 1 edition. Aldershot, Hampshire, England and Burlington, VT: Routledge.

Zein-Elabdin, Eiman. 2001. "Contours of a Non-modernist Discourse: The Contested Space of History and Development." *Review of Radical Political Economy* 33 (3): 255–63.

Zito, Anthony R. 2001. "Epistemic Communities, Collective Entrepreneurship and European Integration." *Journal of European Public Policy* 8 (4): 585–603.

2   La santé avant tout
(Health before everything)

While revolutionaries as individuals can be murdered, you cannot kill ideas.

– Thomas Sankara

This chapter explores ownership, or *l'appropriation de développement*, in Burkina Faso – a former French colony located in West Africa. My analysis is informed by the words and deeds of Thomas Sankara (2007), which help orient this chapter around the complex but practical nature of ideas. Thirty-eight original interviews and participant observation carried out between June and August of 2015 with government officials in the Burkinabe Ministry of Health (MoH) as well as the Ministry of Finance and Economics (MOFE), civil society organizations (CSOs), community-based associations, and international donors aid me in understanding what *l'appropriation de développement* means in Burkina Faso and how it functions. I conducted seven interviews with four different donors working in the health sector: The Peace Corps, World Bank, United Nations Populations Fund (UNFPA), and the U.S. Agency for International Development (USAID). From the Ministry of Health (which includes civil servants working at local clinics) and the Ministry of Finance and Economics, I collected seventeen interviews. Finally, I spoke with fourteen representatives from within civil society. I found that policymakers shared similar understandings of ownership with members of civil society who are involved in the country's health sector. Burkinabe view *l'appropriation de développement* as a collective engagement and individual commitment to developing the country. Representatives of donor institutions, by contrast, grounded their understanding of ownership in a country's financial capabilities: Was the Burkinabe government financing its development? More importantly, this chapter details various social and political outgrowths of the ownership paradigm in Burkina Faso that illustrate the need to rethink the promotion of the paradigm as necessary for emancipatory development.

Investing in the ownership paradigm

International donors and supranational institutions have played a long and sustained role in Burkina Faso's development practices. The Burkinabe health sector is highly demonstrative of the country's history with regional and international institutions. In 1987, the World Health Organization (WHO) and UNICEF developed the Bamako Initiative (BI) as a corrective to the salient inefficiencies in the health sectors across Africa. More specifically, the BI was tailored to address the dearth of resources in many African states as they tried to implement comprehensive primary health programs (see UNICEF n.d.). The Burkinabe government launched its version of the BI in 1993 and, in 1996, reconfigured its health sector, adding regional health districts, creating eleven health regions over fifty-three health districts, as well as implementing cost-sharing mechanisms, like user fees, to generate income for the health sector (Ridde 2011). That initiative reflects some of the core principles of neoliberal development policy recommendations, such as cost-sharing. Within this model, consumers carry the burden of health costs, which in Burkina Faso meant increased cost for essential generic drugs (Haddad, Nougtara, and Fournier 2006). Under the BI, the government also decentralized the health sector (again, with an emphasis on efficiency), the underlying assumption being that communities could better manage the delivery and maintenance of health services than the central government (Ridde 2011). The plan led to the creation of private pharmacy depots that provide generic drugs to health centers at the district level. Another element of the BI was increased reliance on donor funding for the health sector. Donors were encouraged to contribute to the initial purchase of essential generic drugs, and between 1992 and 1998 donor contributions to health increased by about thirty-one percent annually (Haddad, Nougtara, and Fournier 2006, 1891).

Scholars have linked the macroeconomic reforms under World Bank and IMF-instituted structural adjustment programs (SAPs) to the stagnant progress in the public health sector in Africa (Kanji 1989; Ridde 2011; Konadu-Agyemang 2000; Sahn and Bernier 1995). Because of currency devaluation, drug prices became too exorbitant for most Burkinabe. Drug prices increased by seventy-six percent and medication represented about eighty percent of the cost of visiting health professionals, while fees for consultation increased between 100 and 150 percent, and the cost of delivering a baby increased by twenty to thirty percent (Haddad, Nougtara, and Fournier 2006, 1892). After the SAP reforms, health care in Burkina Faso became more expensive than in neighboring countries like Mali and Côte d'Ivoire (Bodart et al. 2001). The population remained generally dissatisfied with health services and the allocation of resources remained inefficient.

These lingering lacunae from the BI implementation and SAPs is attributed to donors and NGOs in the health sector that overemphasized efficiencies at the expense of equity in health (Ridde 2008).

A distinct discourse on international interventions and approaches to development and health in Burkina Faso emerged with the creation of Poverty Reduction Strategy Papers (PRSPs) and the Millennium Development Goals (MDGs) in 1999 and 2000, respectively. As a Heavily Indebted Poor Country (HIPC), Burkina Faso produced its first PRSP, titled *Le Cadre stratégique de lutte contre la pauvreté* (Strategic Framework for the Fight Against Poverty), which was implemented in 2000 (Ministère de l'Economie et des Finances 2000). That same year, Burkina Faso also became a signatory to the MDGs. In making this global pledge to reduce poverty, the government agreed to work towards achieving the eight pre-established development goals, three of which are health-related.[1] The shift in international development discourse to partnership and poverty reduction prompted a call to increase donor funding and presence in national development strategies, along with the mobilization of domestic resources to meet these new development goals. A year after agreeing to work towards the MDGs, Burkina Faso collaborated with a number of other states in the African Union to produce the Abuja Declaration, through which they agreed to allocate at least fifteen percent of their annual budgets to their health sectors. Ideally, in meeting the Abuja pledge, these states would also achieve the three health-related MDGs (World Health Organization 2011). African leaders also called on donors to meet their former pledge of committing at least 0.7 percent of their domestic gross national income (GNI) to development in Africa (World Health Organization 2011). These globally-oriented documents inform the current foci of political and economic resources in the Burkinabe health sector.

Since the early 1990s, the World Bank has facilitated Burkina Faso's transition to a market economy and neoliberalization (World Bank 2013). Beginning with independence in 1960, the government produced five-year development plans that spanned periods from 1967–1971, 1972–1976, 1977–1981, 1986–1990, and 1991–1995. Between 1984 and 1985, the government elaborated the biannual *Programme Populaire de Développement* (PPD, People's Development Program) (Ministère de la Planification et du Développement Populaire 1985). After 1995, the government moved away from five-year plans to its first ten-year strategy. *La lettre d'intention de politique de développement humain durable* (LIPDHD, Letter of Intent on Sustainable Human Development Policy) was the first ten-year development plan that the Burkinabe government established. However, the government quickly jettisoned this plan when it became eligible for HIPC funds in 1997 and had to replace the LIPDHD with the *Cadre stratégique de lutte contre la pauvreté* (CSLP, Strategic Framework for Poverty Reduction) – the country's first PRSP – in 2000. Because the country was under pressure to complete the first CSLP in order to receive HIPC funds, the government created this document in just seven months (World Bank 2013). The CSLP, being the first iteration of the PRSP, was Burkina Faso's comprehensive and long-term approach to social, political, and economic development. It reflected the spirit of the ownership paradigm, expressing a long-term, holistic vision in the language of country-led partnership and ownership, and was results-oriented, meaning it elaborated time-bound targets to measure the achievement of goals. The first CSLP spanned 2000 to 2010. After the CSLP came *La stratégie de croissance accélérée et de développement durable* (SCADD, The Strategy for Accelerated Growth and Sustainable Development), which covered 2011 until 2015.

The SCADD is the second iteration of Burkina Faso's PRSP. Much like the CSLP, the SCADD articulates the present state of development in the economic, political, and social sectors and provides a technocratic strategy for achieving the stated development goals. Like the CSLP, the SCADD takes economic cues from the neoliberal playbook. According to the government and donors, key problems in the health sector include weak governance and leadership, inadequate health service delivery, and insufficient resources to fund health services (World Bank 2011; Organisation Mondiale de la Santé 2009; Ministère de l'Economie et des Finances 2011). The SCADD grounds development successes in country ownership and increased donor assistance, to be realized through six core principles: Forecasting, country ownership, accountability, sustainable development, coordinating actions, and results-based management (Ministère de l'Economie et des Finances 2011, 35). The government goes on to define ownership, or *l'appropriation nationale*, as the government and other national actors' commitment to lead the process of elaboration and implementation of national development strategies and policies in line with the priorities and needs of the population. Attaining ownership involves the effective coordination and use of official development assistance, taking into account the comparative advantages offered by each technical and financial partner (Ministère de l'Economie et des Finances 2011, 35).

Through a formal adoption of the discourse and donor-sanctioned tools and instruments for development, the Burkinabe government has consented to the principles and practices of the ownership paradigm. The adoption of the CSLP and SCAAD as long-term, holistic development strategies that define development in terms of poverty reduction through economic growth comes directly from the World Bank, not the Burkinabe contexts. The consequences of the government's acceptance of the ownership paradigm unfold across the range of Burkinabe development stakeholders, prescribing and locking in their relative positions and values towards national development.

Top-down development

A number of significant themes come to light through examination of ownership at the national level, which in turn reveal how this concept is understood by community-level CSOs in the Burkinabe health sector. I found little consistency across stakeholders on what ownership means, how it is executed, and whether it even exists in Burkina Faso's health sector. For various donor stakeholders included in this study, such as the World Bank, the U.S. Peace Corps, United Nations Population Fund, and USAID, ownership was very much about the government and local stakeholders taking the lead with respect to funding development and participating in program implementation. For example, one respondent in the World Bank's country office in Burkina Faso stated, "ownership of development in the health sector is the Ministry of Health giving all the resources that it has, both technical and financial, to meet development partners halfway; not just the Ministry of Health, the communities as well."[2] Another donor from USAID noted that who owns development is "whoever contributes most of the budget."[3]

Donors

Although donors mentioned contributing to Burkina Faso's Plan National de Développement Sanitaire (PNDS) and "accompanying" the government in its quest to execute the stated objectives, no donor (other than one World Bank official) used the document as an example of government ownership (Ministère de la Santé 2011). That the Bank employee quoted above highlighted the government's creation of the PNDS as evidence of government ownership of development is not striking, particularly because the Bank is responsible for formulating and promoting this technocratic approach to development policy-making (Pender 2001; Goldman 2006). The Bank is heavily invested in the government's ownership of the PNDS. However, this particular Bank representative also linked ownership to the government's ability to finance 100 percent of the health sector – and development programs and projects overall:

> Avec la déclaration de Paris, on peut dire qu'il y a un tendance vers l'appropriation. Bien sûr, quand tu as 40 pour cent de ton financement qui dépend des aides extérieurs, tu peux avoir petites influences par ci, par là. (With the Paris Declaration one can say there is a trend towards ownership. Of course, when you have 40 percent of your financing dependent on outside aid, you can expect small influences here and there.)[4]

Notably, respondents at the World Bank did not see the Burkinabe government as fully owning development in the health sector, but rather as being on track to do so.

Government

For government officials in the MOFE, specifically the subdivision known as the *Direction générale de l'économie et de la planification* (DGEP), ownership is a combination of control over policies and engagement with development. The element of control over policies seems informed by the hegemonic version of ownership in that several respondents used the "government in the driver's seat" metaphor to define the concept. Aspects of the hegemonic version of ownership are also evident in the reasons why most of these actors believe that government does in fact own development. For civil servants in the DGEP, government owns development because it takes the initiative in creating national documents, like the SCADD and CSLP. In the MoH, there is a connection between ownership and engagement, and policy-makers across the board view ownership as involving an engaged awareness about development. The expected level of engaged awareness percolates down to the individual level where, as one official noted, "Chacun a son part à jouer." (Everyone has a role to play.)[5] But more importantly, each person knows what her/his part is. A sense of responsibility and independence seeps through this understanding: "Nous devons écrire les chemins que nous voulons suivre." (We must write the paths we want to follow.)[6]

Whether these same actors see the government as "owning" development is nuanced. Government respondents at the local level, including nurses and midwives working at the health center in Koudougou believe that government owns development based the allotment of government subsidies for services and medication and the decentralized state of health care, a process over which they feel they have little control. In response to my question as to whether or not the government owns development, technocrats in the MoH suggested otherwise. One top government official in the MoH gave a resounding, No!

> Non, le gouvernement ne s'approprie pas le développement parce que le gouvernement détruire l'argent. Il gaspille l'argent. Ça veut dire qu'ils travaillent, oui, mais ce n'est pas arrivé. Ils auraient pu mieux faire. (No, the government does not own development because the government wastes money. That means they work, yes, but it's not enough. They should have done better.)[7]

For other officials in the MoH, the reason for government not owning development came back to the question of aid dependence. "Il y a beaucoup de volonté pour pouvoir aller dans le sens de [l'appropriation], mais quand on n'a pas souvent l'argent, les choses sont dicter d'ailleurs, quoi." (There's a lot of will to own development, but when one doesn't have money, these things are controlled from elsewhere.)[8]

Burkinabe government officials were particularly proud of, and grounded in, their national and sector-wide strategy for health promotion, the PNDS.[9] One official in the MoH maintained,

> je me dit que le Burkina s'approprie son développement; par exemple, je prends le PNDS. Un peu en Afrique d'Ouest [le Burkina] est un exemple. Le Burkina est un exemple et les gens même viens s'inspirer de l'exemple de Burkina. (Burkina owns its development, for example, take the PNDS. Burkina is somewhat of an example in West Africa. Burkina is an example and people are even inspired by Burkina.)[10]

Pointing out how Burkina Faso's PNDS is an example that other West African states emulate for their own health strategies reveals the pride some Burkinabe government officials take in having elaborated these operational strategies. One Burkinabe doctor whom I interviewed, who currently works for USAID but formerly practiced under the MoH, characterized the PNDS as an important document that the government elaborated to achieve strategic objectives in the health sector.[11] At the same time, another top USAID official (who happened to be American) described the document as not that important and not a living document because there had been no changes to the PNDS since it was validated.[12] The official Burkinabe rendering of ownership accepts the government's pride and commitment to PNDS as an example of the state owning development.

Civil society organizations

Burkina Faso's civil society comprises a large, vibrant array of actors. Some scholars have mislabeled Burkinabe civil society as apolitical, when in fact citizens have engaged in a number of politically transformative movements (Engberg-Pedersen 2002). Since 2008, multiple movements (both organized and acephalous) steeped in political and economic demands have arisen around issues ranging from cost of living to police impunity (Harsch 2016; Sangaré and Vink 2015). Calls by the international community for the inclusion of CSOs in the development process and as stakeholders in the ownership model come against this backdrop of considerable domestic political unrest (OECD 2008, 2011). Donors continue to expect that civil society organizations and people will increase the government's potential for achieving development goals in the health sector (Brinkerhoff 1999; Steinle and Correll 2008), regardless of the level of internal unrest.

A plethora of actors contributes to the Burkinabe health system: Faith-based organizations, nongovernmental organizations, international nongovernment organizations, and CSOs, to name just a few. Under the ownership paradigm, these actors should participate in elaborating the sector-wide health strategy and aid government in implementing the projects and programs tied to national health policies. For example, community members elect representatives from their villages to serve on *Comités de Gestion* (CoGes, Management Committee), which are responsible for implementing health-related activities and using funds collected from the community in conjunction with the Centre de Santé et Promotion Sociale (CSPS). Community members are also responsible for selecting the manager of the pharmacy from within the community. With a decentralized health system based on the Bamako Initiative, local actors are heavily incorporated into the health framework, but whether they in fact exercise power or have autonomy is an altogether different question, to which I will return.

Civil society members also play a critical role in implementing the policies and programs tied to either the national health strategy or donor health programs and projects that circumvent that strategy. For example, to implement the *Programme d'Appui au Développement Sanitaire* (PADS, Program to Support Health Development) and the PNDS, donors and government fund large NGOs that, in turn, find local associations throughout a particular region to implement the different activities and persuade (*sensibiliser*, in French) the population to accept new health norms, based on PADS directives. These community-based organizations are responsible for working with a certain number of villages and their *agents de santé* (health promoters) to carry out grassroots health promotion in the village. In this way, civil society members become essential to implementing health policies created under the ownership model, in a top-down fashion that also appears to be bottom-up. This diffusion model shows that ownership is not an innocuous concept that state actors and donors employ with little consequence. Instead, civil society actors breathe life into the concept through their implementation of PADS and other national health strategies produced under the ownership framework.

The CSO actors whom I interviewed defined ownership using a sentiment similar to what government officials voiced. Respondents in the different community-based organizations, and in civil society in general, often met my question, "What does ownership of development mean to you?" with hesitation. I often had to explain that there was no right answer to the question. Collectively, civil society members working in the health sector relate ownership to an understanding of the role that individuals within the community have in bringing about development at the country level:

> Le développement droit être un problème ou une question de tout le monde. Et tout le monde droit s'impliquer pour que l'Etat puisse se développer. Ce n'est pas un problème de seulement les dirigeants pour le gouvernement, mais tous les citoyens s'impliquer pour qu'on puisse atteindre ce développement effectivement. (Development should be a problem or a question for everyone. And everyone should involve himself or herself so that the state can develop. It's not a problem for only government leaders, but all citizens should help towards development.)[13]

These sentiments reflect the dominant understanding of development amongst members of civil society.

> L'appropriation de développement, ça veut dire que chacun de nous a en tête son développement. Il ne droit pas attendre que quelqu'un ailleurs pour venir te dire, il faut que tu fasses comme ça pour être développer. Ça, ce n'est pas un développement qui est propre à toi même. (Ownership of development means that each one of us has development in mind. He shouldn't wait for someone from elsewhere to tell you, "You must do it this way in order to be developed." This is not a development that is unique to you.)[14]

For many people in civil society, notions of ownership are thus shaped both by the need to understand the policy itself and by a felt sense of responsibility for implementing it.

As with many government officials, many civil society respondents do believe that the government owns development in the health sector because it produces development strategies for the sector. One respondent working for a local association in Tenkodogo stated, "le gouvernement essaye de s'approprier le développement parce que le gouvernement a élaboré ces plans de développement." (The government tries to own development because it elaborated its development plans.)[15] Not all civil society members felt that government was either owning or on track to own development in the health sector, however. For many, especially those not working with PADS or NGOs, the government was not in a position to own development because of the democratic transition that was taking place at the time (i.e. in the summer of 2015). Again, the consensus across civil society was that government was on course to own development, not because it was fully funding development in the health sector but because it had created the health strategies and works with donors.

How does ownership work in Burkina Faso?

As I explained in Chapter one, ownership should ameliorate the aid relationship between aid-receiving governments and donors. The paradigm makes clear the necessity of partnership among all development stakeholders so that foreign aid is more efficient in producing development outcomes. Accordingly, governments must work towards ownership: It is a process. Nevertheless, ownership should mark a break from earlier iterations of neoliberal development in which donors were the central actors and knowers of development. In Burkina Faso, the language and practice of ownership do not reflect a clear demarcation from previous donor-led development. Instead, I found that aspects of the paradigm entrench many of the problematic tenets of neoliberal development. In this section, I detail how under this paradigm, the Burkinabe whom I interviewed in the government and civil society collectively referred to themselves and the country as underdeveloped, despite its having higher indicators of progress than other African countries. I also explain how the results-based approach that is essential to ownership constrains and shapes CBO practices around health care in that it requires CBOs to become professionalized in a grammar and practice that orients their priorities away from the communities they aim to serve. In the end, the considerable influence that donors continue to exert under the ownership paradigm comes without a mechanism for holding them accountable.

Feeling underdeveloped

In 2015, the year I conducted fieldwork, Burkina Faso had been trying to "own" development for fifteen years, since the first PRSP was drafted in 2000. Before ever adopting a PRSP or using the language of ownership, Burkinabe had been operating donor-led development plans, at least since 1987 when Sankara died and Blaise Compaoré came to power. Despite this long engagement with development plans and strategies, the Burkinabe whom I interviewed consider themselves and the country to still be underdeveloped.

At the state level, the Burkinabe government has tangibly bought into the notion that the country is underdeveloped, or developing, by producing PRSPs. One government official went so far as to say,

> L'Europe ne nous aide pas. L'Amérique ne nous aide pas. On ne va jamais se développer parce qu'eux aussi, ils ont travaillé pour le

développement. (Europe doesn't help us. America doesn't help us. We will never develop because they [Europe and America] also worked for their development.)[16]

Another government official noted,

> Le Burkina, c'est un pays sous-développé. Donc, quand on parle de développement, c'est de sortir de sous-développement. . . . C'est d'être totalement indépendant. Actuellement, on dépend beaucoup de l'aide extérieur. (Burkina is an underdeveloped country. When one speaks of development, it's to get out of being underdeveloped. . . . It's to be totally independent. Right now, we depend a lot on outside aid.)[17]

No government official would disagree with this statement. In fact, these sentiments resurfaced at the MOFE and MoH alike, with government officials describing Burkina Faso as "un pays pauvre" (a poor country) or "un pays sous-développé" (an underdeveloped country).[18] Civil society actors were also keen to point out how poor and underdeveloped the country is. Health workers in various associations articulated a very similar sentiment to that voiced by government officials:

> On ne peut pas dire actuellement que le Burkina se développe même. Mais il y a des efforts qui sont fait qu'a même pour aller vers ce développement-là. (We can't actually say that Burkina is developing right now. But at least there are efforts being made towards development.)[19]

The figures below paint a different picture. Burkina Faso has been making substantial progress on many of the indicators deemed essential for development of the health sector under the ownership paradigm. For example, out-of-pocket contributions dropped significantly between 2000 and 2010, even though the government provides a higher percentage towards the health expenditure compared to the average African country and other low-income countries (Pande, Leive, Smitz, Eozenou, Ozcelik 2013). Burkina Faso has also averaged higher growth rates and lower inflation than the average low-income countries and the average African country between 2012 and 2017 (Pande et al. 2013). These are not the sole indicators of modern development, although they figure prominently into modern conceptualizations of progress. Why Burkinabe continue to see themselves as underdeveloped in their quest to own development is unclear. Post-development scholars posit that the development industry *ipso facto* demands an underdeveloped subject in order to legitimate itself (Escobar 1995; Ferguson 1994; Sachs 1992). Because the ownership paradigm does not disrupt the power discourses internal to the history of development, but instead maintains them in reconfigured forms, it seems likely that for Burkinabe stakeholders to be vested in ownership, they would first have to see themselves and the state of their development as lagging but for donor financing and technical assistance (Wynter 1996).

This sense of underdevelopment may also come from the ownership paradigm's configuration of donors as experts and knowledge sources responsible for building local capacity. For example, one staff member I interviewed in the Burkina Faso office of the World Bank related how "la Banque joue un rôle de *knowledge* génération" (the Bank plays the role of knowledge generation).[20] Donors' positioning as sources of knowledge for health development is also evident in their strategies for health, which, as each respondent put it, are to "reinforce" either capacity or the health system. However, the tacit assumption is that Burkinabe do not yet possess the capacity to build strong institutions or the knowledge to develop. To counter this assumption, one need only look at Yacouba Sawadogo, who was able to reverse desertification in a part of Northern Burkina Faso using traditional farming techniques – a feat that donors and other so-called experts could not achieve (Dodd 2010).

Measurable development

Results-based development is integral to the ownership process (OECD 2011; Wolfensohn and Fischer 2000). As such, it is one of the six guiding principles in the SCADD. The Burkinabe government states that results-based management aims to meet the objectives and indicators outlined in the national strategy by making each actor accountable for working towards these ends and clearly articulating the process for implementing the outlined development activities (Ministère de l'Economie et des Finances 2011, 36). One of the ways this happens in the health sector is by having community-based organizations carry out programs in conjunction with the local health clinics. While in Tenkodogo, I observed a how the focus on measurable results under ownership dictates the rapport between local associations and funding agencies so that the CBO's become accountable to NGOs and donors, not their own communities.

I observed a meeting with the NGO *Renforcement de Capacités* (REN-CAP) and ten CBOs working in Tenkodogo in July 2015. RENCAP funds these associations as they implement health programming in line with targets outlined in the PADS. The targets in the PADS come directly from the PNDS, which is informed by the SCADD. Funding and targets come not just from the government through these national strategies but also from donors who comprise the *pannier commun* (community basket), a group of donors, including the World Bank, UNFPA, and GAVI Vaccination. The donors funded four strategic activities: Improving governance and leadership in health, reinforcing communication to change behavior, improving delivery of health services, and promoting health and the fight against diseases. These donors and the government pay RENCAP to manage and pay the CBOs. The CBOs report on their progress towards meeting the targets outlined in the PADS and by the *pannier commun* to RENCAP, which then gathers the data for a larger report to transmit to the donors and government. At the meeting I attended, the associations reported their progress on the four strategic activities from January through June 2015.

The tone and orientation of the meeting illustrates the impact of donor priorities and knowledge structures on how policies are executed and subsequently turned into reports that suggest progress in development. The number of activities around changing behavior weighed heavily in whether the RENCAP thought the associations would continue to receive funding. In fact, at one point, a number of associations had to explain why they were not able to execute the *perdue de vue* activity that was specifically paid for by GAVI Vaccinations.[21] Most of the association members attributed their inability to complete the task to the lack of cooperation from the head nurses at the CSPS, along with the last-minute addition of GAVI to the list of participants. In response, the head of the NGO emphasized that the associations' failure to complete the task and spend the money would lead to less money for the CBOs in the future. During the break, one association member expressed frustration with the process, stating,

> quand un financement tombe, ce n'est pas pour s'amuser avec. On vous dit, voilà, vous respectez nos clauses. Nous voulons intervenir dans le district sanitaire de Tenkodogo. Et voilà, nous attendons telle, telle, et telle résultats. Donc, c'est [les partenaires technique et financier (PTF)] qui a le dernier mot. Nous, on ne fait qu'exécuter leur désires, quoi. (When you lose financing, it's not something to play with. [Donors] tell you, look, you respect our terms. We want to work in Tenkodogo's health district. And we expect these, these, and these results. So, it's the donors who have the last word. Us, we just do what they want.)[22]

The precarious nature of funding structures the activities and services CBOs provide to their communities while simultaneously professionalizing the associations (Hickey 2012). As the director of one association noted, "on est dans un système où le financement est obligatoire. On a un besoin de financement pour pouvoir fonctionner." (We are in a system where financing is necessary. We need funds to function.) Or, as another member of a different association stated, "aujourd'hui, on comprend, . . . ça évolue avec l'argent." (Today, things evolve with money.)[23] This sense of financial necessity guides much of the reverence for donors and their contributions to the health sector. Many of the association members opined how their organizations could not continue functioning without funds from the PADS. The head of one association mentioned, for example,

> deux fois, il y a des difficultés parce que les activités que vous avez pré-vue après le financement, vous n'arrivez pas à réaliser tous les activi-tés prévue. Après la défense du projet, on vous loue un montant. On vous finance un montant et vous êtes obligé de diminuer les activités. (Sometimes it's difficult because the activities that you have planned, after receiving the funding you can't achieve all of the activities you've planned. After defending the cost of the projects, you're given an amount. You're given an amount and you're obligated to reduce your activities.)[24]

Simultaneously, all the associations expressed that they needed donor funding to keep their doors open. However, it was clear that many were driven not by the need to receive donor funding, but to serve their communi-ties, and although they would have a difficult time doing so without donors, they were often looking for ways to make the seemingly divergent interests overlap. Often this happened around health concerns like family planning. When there were no overlapping interests, financial considerations com-pelled the associations to work towards the donor and government targets to demonstrate to donors that their strategies were working.

Influence with impunity

Government officials were very clear that the Burkinabe government elab-orates its own health development strategies in collaboration with other stakeholders (both local and international). Again, this exemplified owner-ship for many of the respondents in the MOFE and MoH. However, they also made it very clear that developing and executing the strategies would be especially difficult without donors' financial and technical assistance.[25] For example, nurses at the CSPS in Koudougou were vocal about the role they think donors play in keeping the health system afloat: "C'est eux qui vient justement soulager beaucoup plus la population Burkinabè." (It's donors who come and relieve so much of the Burkinabe population.)[26] More often than not, health workers suggested that donor influence and presence were not only positive but essential for providing subsidized medicines and ser-vices to the population. My own observations at a typical CSPS confirmed the ubiquitous presence of donors. The building and aesthetics were by no means welcoming. Parts of the ceiling were rotted out. All the walls were covered with more dirt than paint. The floors, cracked slabs of cement, were equally layered in dirt. Each wall displayed health propaganda that bore the mark of an international donor. One sign, paid for by USAID, stated, "You want your wife to help you work? Support her in choosing a contraceptive." Each of the consultation rooms contained boxes of Plumpy Nut and sacks of cereal from World Food Program, staples of food relief. Given the amount of tangible goods the nurses at the CSPS receive from donors and the ubiquitous presence of donor-sponsored health fliers, it is no wonder they feel that donors maintain the health system.

The visible influence of key donors in the health sector does not automatically translate into equal partnership with respect to accountability. USAID and the World Health Organization are two of the most prominent donors in the health sector, and in Burkina Faso, they are two of the most guarded and difficult donors to access, in contrast to government offices. I could only wonder how any civil society actor in the country could feel like an equal partner with donors, especially when few had access to donor personnel and resources. More importantly, donors' physical inaccessibility mirrors how unreachable they are when it comes to accountability.

Instead of saying outright that donors are funding the health sector or dictating the policy direction, some government officials I interviewed used the term *accompagner* (to accompany), which is integral to the language of ownership. Donors exist only to accompany the government by providing technical and financial expertise.

> Les PTF n'ont pas d'influence comme ça sur le PNDS. Oui, ils ont participé à l'élaboration de PNDS. Alors, comme nous sommes un pays a ressource limiter, il n'y a pas beaucoup d'argent, ce sont des partenaires maintenant qui nous aident. . . . Ils pourront qu'accompagner. (Donors don't have that much influence over the PNDS. Yes, they helped to elaborate the PNDS. Since we are a country with limited resources, there isn't a lot of money. It's the partners now who come and help us [but] they only accompany us.)[27]

As I probed further in interviews in an effort to have officials explain how donors are merely accompanying government when they also provided the framework for the PNDS, *panier commun*, and PRSPs (initially approving all of these documents before work could commence), respondents began to speak more candidly about the ways in which donors influence health policies.

> Puis que c'est eux qui finance la mise en œuvre de ces documents. Donc les PTF même s'approprie plus nos documents que nous-même. Voilà,

ils ont travaillé beaucoup avec les PTF de PNUD, le système de Nations Unis en générale. Mais ils connaissent bien nos documents, oui. (Donors finance the implementation of these documents. The PTFs own our documents more than we do. They work a lot with donors from UNDP, the UN system in general. But they are very familiar with our documents.)[28]

This explanation focuses on the financial influence that donors wield over the policy process. Indeed, when respondents did acknowledge donor influence, it was primarily financial. Even if they wanted to implement alternative projects or programs in the health sector, they felt that the process would be futile since the government does not have the economic resources to pay for health projects and programs without donor support. The reality is that donors will only pay for a development project that corresponds with their vision. For example, USAID was clear about its lack of support for traditional medicine and any health intervention not approved by the WHO, despite traditional medicine being incorporated into the Burkinabe government's national health strategy.[29]

Despite their influence over health policies in Burkina Faso, donors still maintain that they have limited influence over development. As one World Bank official characterized the situation, donors have only as much influence as the government allows.[30] In fact, this same official suggested that bilateral donors like the U.S. were more likely to push their own agendas to influence health policies than the multilateral donors:

[M]ais l'influence sur le développement de pays n'est pas obligatoirement les multilatéraux telle que la Banque Mondial et le FMI. L'influence est beaucoup plus votre pays, les pays bilatéraux. C'est eux qui font l'influence de développement et empêche l'appropriation en tant que telle. (But the influence over country development is not necessarily the multilaterals such as the World Bank and IMF. The influence is much more your country, the bilateral countries like France, Germany, and the United States. They are the ones that influence development and impede ownership as such.)[31]

While there may be more overt political agendas with bilateral donors (which seemed to be the case especially with USAID), the World Bank and IMF's ability to dictate the direction of health policies in Burkina Faso may be more pernicious because it is not so overt (Goldman 2006). Surprisingly enough, another World Bank officer professed,

We go into a meeting with the ministry and they express the need to, I don't know, um, revise a law or something. We will supply them with the technical support, but there's a conflict of interest there because we actually want the law to change, so we will channel the technical support not toward the views of the ministry but from our own perspective. And so, you wonder, where is the ownership at that point?[32]

By measuring ownership with respect to PRSPs and funding mechanisms, there is no space to discuss the embedded presence of donors in the policy and development process; this, in turn, makes deciphering whether government and local stakeholders are in control of development both tedious and difficult. Or, as James Ferguson aptly notes,

We will not have a balanced understanding of the actual processes through which Africa is governed until we move beyond the myth of the sovereign African nation-state to explore the powerful but almost wholly unaccountable transnational institutions that effectively (and often not so effectively) rule large domains of African economy and society.

(2006, 87)

The emphasis placed on knowledge production and reinforcing capacity speaks directly to the limitations of the ownership paradigm: There is no language or practice for holding donors accountable. As such, the demand for ownership does not fully depart from previous development paradigms that centered donors as knowers and defenders of development. This is especially evident in how the words and deeds of the epistemic community of donors and Burkinabe stakeholders' dependence on donors shape family planning policies and their implementation.

Family planning and ownership

According to international donors like UNFPA, USAID, and The Bill and Melinda Gates Foundation, the negative impact of limited access to family planning on both global and domestic economies places this issue within the scope of development. Family planning is purportedly one more technically complicated problem deemed too difficult for African governments to address without financial and technical expertise from donors (Ajong et al. 2016; May 2016), but Burkinabe development stakeholders do engage in the arena where knowledge, family planning, and economics intersect. The SCADD states that the fifty-nine percent of the population under twenty years of age imposes an untenable strain on country, noting that it is the poorer communities that have the most children, which keeps these families in poverty (Ministère de l'Economie et des Finances 2011, 9).

In Burkina Faso's *National Family Planning Stimulus Plan 2013–2015*, the government warns that unchecked population growth to fifty-five million people by 2050 would mean excessive strain on resources, leading to limited employment options and stalled poverty reduction (Burkina Faso, MoH n.d., 7), and that maternal deaths could be reduced by up to thirty percent through family planning. Implementing the population policies will be a matter of private-public partnerships, getting men involved, and monitoring availability of contraceptives (Burkina Faso, MoH, n.d.). The fight to provide access to contraceptives in Burkina Faso necessitates generating a demand for them. Some 1.5 million people in rural areas do not want to space out or limit births; another 280,000 want to but do not want family planning, compared to 160,000 women in rural Burkina Faso who want to space out their births but are limited in their understanding of family planning. Similar disparities are also evident in urban areas: 280,000 women do not want to space or limit births; 70,000 want to, but not through family planning, while only 40,000 want to space out their births but are not knowledgeable about family planning (Burkina Faso, MoH n.d., 11). The high number of women in Burkina Faso who do not want to space or limit births indicates that there is little demand for modern contraceptives.

Donors and the government attribute the limited demand for modern contraceptives and spacing of births to traditional commitments at the local level, and this shapes approaches to community health. *Sensibilisation*, or consciousness-raising, is an attempt to change an individual or community's comportment around a given issue, and it can take a number of forms, such as talks, individual interviews, movies, and demonstrations of products. The underlying assumption is that the original behavior is detrimental to the individual's livelihood or the community, so community health associations employ consciousness-raising strategies around family planning to persuade people that not using modern contraceptives and/or spacing births is symptomatic of tradition and underdevelopment. As one health agent noted, "Notre objectif c'est d'amener cette population à laisser tomber ces choses traditionnelle." (Our objective is to get this population to let go of traditional things.)[33] In fact, the local associations' primary responsibilities are to inculcate in the surrounding communities the policies being paid for under the PADS.

Local actors take their orders directly from the national development strategy, which is largely the product of donor and international priorities in conjunction with government-identified priorities, which align with the larger development paradigm. The World Bank requires the NGOs and local associations receiving money from the PADS to instill in men and women an understanding of the advantages of family planning through sixteen targeted training modules.[34]

Shaming women into adopting modern forms of family planning thus becomes integral to development. The director of one of the associations remarked with conviction,

> C'est une fonction de ça qu'au niveau des OMD . . . mais le Burkina, ne sera pas au rendez-vous. On n'a pas atteint parce que jusqu' aujourd'hui il y a des décès maternels. Si je vous sors les résultats tout de suite vous allez voir qu'à Tenkodogo il y a eu plus de vingt décès maternels aux cours de l'année 2014. A donc, c'est pour dire que ce n'est pas fini, la planification familiale. Une femme, neuf enfants, c'est trop. Ou bien? (It's a matter of the MDGs . . . but Burkina will not meet the MDGs. We didn't reach the goals because today there is still maternal mortality. If I showed you the numbers, you would see that in Tenkodogo there were more than twenty maternal deaths in 2014. That means that we are not done with family planning. One woman, nine children, that's too much, right?)[35]

This statement reveals how the MDGs filter from the international level into the communities. The director frames Burkina Faso's progress in terms of reaching the MDGs and, in line with ownership, blames failure to decrease maternal mortality rates on women's failure to adopt family planning. He continued,

> la planification n'a pas marché. La population n'a pas compris. Et il y a un grand travail à faire pour que la population puisse comprendre . . . parce que quand tu regard, il y a trop de décès infantile. Le taux est élevé. Alors, dans autres pays, et quand tu fais la comparaison, tu vois la Belgique le taux de décès est trop bas au niveau maternel. (Planning did not work. The population did not understand. And there is a great deal of work to be done so that the public can understand . . . because when you look, there are too many infant deaths. The rate is high. In other countries, and when you make the comparison, you see Belgium, the maternal death rate is much lower.)[36]

For this official, the need to *understand* the importance of family planning is lost on the local population in a way that it is not in Belgium, where maternal death rates are low. Once again, the inability to develop is constructed as internal to the Burkinabe, not the consequence of inequities in the valuation of knowledge or unbalanced global economic structures.

This type of thinking was pervasive across development stakeholders I surveyed, but especially those actors working closely with communities. For example, another health agent working in a rural community explained,

> Nous au Burkina, ici, on met beaucoup au monde des enfants. Tu vas trouver une famille qui a douze, treize enfants, la seule femme. Alors que le monsieur peut avoir trois ou quatre femmes. Si chaque femme a douze enfants, lui seul, il a combiné plus de trente, quarante et l'entretien est difficile. . . . Donc, on sensibiliser surtout si c'est la planification familiale pour qu'on diminue le nombre d'enfants qu'on met au monde pour pouvoir les entretenir. (We, in Burkina Faso, we bring a lot of children into the world. You will find a family that has twelve, thirteen children, only one woman. While the gentleman may have three or four women. If every woman has twelve children, he alone has more than thirty, forty, and their maintenance is difficult. . . . So, we have to raise awareness, especially around family planning so that we can reduce the number of children we give birth to, to be able to maintain them.)[37]

Here we see how through the larger policies and approaches to family planning, family size and birthing become understood in the context of productivity within the larger national economy (Murphy 2017).

By suggesting that if Burkina Faso were to reach the projected population rate suggested in the *National Family Planning Stimulus Plan* there would be untenable strain on already limited resources, the government and donors overlook the ways in which resources are strained because they have either been privatized and/or are not being distributed equitably. Scholars have long exposed the fallacy of statements regarding "food scarcity" or lack of access to potable water as natural phenomena (Holt-Giménez et al. 2012; Lappe, Collins, and Fowler 1981; Gleick 2000). Furthermore, the neo-Malthusian approach continues to re-postulate population as a problem solvable only in the realm of economics (Murphy 2017; Hawkesworth 2012). For example, I observed (and mentioned earlier) that donors like USAID and RESPOND Project prominently display posters on local clinic walls encouraging contraception so that women can enter the formal economy. This approach, which is guided by a concern for result-based development and national ownership, atomizes impediments to development at the gender and class levels. In other words, it is poor Burkinabe women who stifle the country's development.

The crisis of overpopulation drives the methods for family planning. And because the OECD's articulation of ownership advocates more concentrated incorporation of international agendas into domestic development frameworks, when donors instill the need to meet international benchmarks like MDGs, they further implant family planning as a norm by mobilizing around reduced maternal mortality. At the national level, when governments take responsibility for these commitments based on the assumption that the problems are not exogenous to the country but internally produced, people at the local level must also fall into line with the given policies. By forcing the population to change its mentality and engage with family planning, the implicit reasoning is that not doing so stalls national progress towards development.

Conclusion

In many respects, the story of ownership in Burkina Faso is the narrative of struggle and sacrifice for the chimera of development. The World Bank, IMF, and international community writ large proposed ownership of development as the panacea for poverty reduction and all-around progress, when, in fact, it proves to be one more nostrum that serves mostly to further entrench donor presence. In my field study of how ownership operates in the Burkinabe health sector, I discovered significant differences across three dominant groups of stakeholders – government, civil society, and donors – specifically, in relation to how these actors define and measure ownership.

Burkinabe development stakeholders view ownership as the individual understanding his or her role or contribution to the overall progress of the community or country. In this way, the civil society representatives and government officials I interviewed produce a conceptualization of ownership informed by their particular experiences with collective progress. However, this version of ownership conflicts with the definition embedded in the ownership paradigm. Consequently, government officials recognize the limitations of ownership as promulgated by the international community of donors. Nevertheless, the Burkinabe government consents to the paradigm in exchange for the development it promises.

Donors continue to assess levels of ownership (whether by government institutions, CSOs, or communities) based on indicators of economic development. And although donors are very influential in the health sector (so much so that many respondents in my interviews believed that the health system would collapse without them), they place responsibility for failed health policies, projects, and programs squarely on the shoulders of the government and individuals unwilling to become "developed." Donors evade responsibility by constructing themselves as "knowledge experts" who are in the country merely to reinforce capacity and accompany Burkina Faso on its path towards development. Consequently, the "knowledge" that these "experts" bring to the health sector, and development in general, creates a different type of dependence that transcends traditional notions of aid-dependence. Donor knowledge is grounded in the assumption that there are no alternative approaches to, or understandings of health and progress that emanate from the Burkinabe themselves. A secondary assumption is that Burkina Faso will attain a certain level of socio-economic progress not based on the resources it has at its disposal but commensurate with the level of outside support it receives. Based on this model, substantial progress will remain elusive; superficial success will come at the expense of alternative knowledge/approaches to development.

The ways in which ownership constructs donors as an infallible source of development knowledge are borne out in Burkina Faso's family planning policies. Global discourses surrounding family planning elicit both real and imagined fears that are ostensibly addressed by developing the underdeveloped. The looming catastrophe around population growth and family planning creates a space for the epistemic community of donors to operate indefinitely. Across Africa, donors and scholars consistently refer to the prevalence and usage of contraceptives as "critical" for economic development (Epstein 2011; Reed 2016). Funding for implementing and monitoring family planning policies in Burkina Faso depends on donors and community-based organizations working with the government. Still, the rhetoric on the ground points to poor women as responsible Burkina's inability to develop because they contribute to unmitigated population growth. Centering poor women and their reproductive choices as detrimental to the country's economic development is one example of the coloniality essential to maintaining ownership and the prominence of the scientific capitalism that informs it.

Notes

1 The Millennium Development Goals were to be attained by 2015. Three of the MDGs pertain to health: MDG number four is to reduce the under-five child mortality rate by two-thirds; number five is to reduce the maternal mortality rate by three-quarters; and, number six is to combat HIV/AIDS, malaria and other diseases.
2 ST0731, 07/31/2015_Ouagadougou.
3 LB0709, 07/09/2015_Ouagadougou.
4 HO0701, 07/01/2015_Ouagadougou.
5 YA1607, 07/16/2015_Koudougou.
6 BS3006, 06/30/2015_Ouagadougou.
7 OB2207, 07/22/2015_Ouagadougou.
8 CD0707, 07/07/2015_Ouagadougou.
9 PNDS is the national strategy that articulates the national plan for developing the health sector, which corresponds with the country's larger economic development objectives in the SCADD, Burkina's PRSP.
10 DR0107, 07/01/2015_Ouagadougou.

11 CM0907, 07/09/2015_Ouagadougou.
12 LB0907, 07/09/2015_Ouagadougou.
13 ZD0308, 08/03/2015_Ouagadougou.
14 ZJ2807, 07/28/2015_Tenkodogo.
15 Ibid.
16 OB2207, 07/22/2015_Ouagadougou.
17 NM0107, 07/01/2015_Koudougou.
18 BS3006, 06/30/2015_Ouagadougou; NM0107, 07/01/2015_Koudougou; DR0107, 07/01/2015_Ouagadougou; CD0707, 07/07/2015_Ouagadougou.
19 ZD0308, 08/03/2015_Tenkodogo.
20 HO0107, 07/01/2015_Ouagadougou.
21 *Perdue de vue* refers to children who do not complete the series of vaccinations. One of the activities that GAVI Vaccination required from members of the local associations was to find these children and keep their names on file.
22 YB0729, 07/29/2015_Tenkodogo.
23 ZJ2807, 07/28/2015_Tenkodogo; KN2707, 07/27/2015_Tenkodogo.
24 SM2407, 24/07/2015_Tenkodogo.
25 OB2207, 07/22/2015_Ouagadougou.
26 RJ1607, 07/16/2015_Koudougou.
27 DR0107, 07/01/2015_Ouagadougou.
28 YS2406, 06/24/2015_Ouagadougou.
29 LB0907, 07/09/2015_Ouagadougou.
30 HO0107, 07/01/2015_Ouagadougou.
31 Ibid.
32 ST0731, 07/31/2015_Ouagadougou.
33 BS2507, 25/07/2015_Tenkodogo.
34 *Rapports du Première Semestre 2015 SOS-ASD Tenkodogo* (The first semester report 2015). This is the Association SOS Santé et Développement's activity for report for RENCAP.
35 KN2707, 27/07/2015_Tenkodogo.
36 Ibid.
37 SM2407, 24/07/2015_Tenkodogo.

References

Ajong, Atem Bethel, Philip Nana Njotang, Martin Ndinakie Yakum, Marie José Essi, Felix Essiben, Filbert Eko Eko, Bruno Kenfack, and Enow Robinson Mbu. 2016. "Determinants of Unmet Need for Family Planning among Women in Urban Cameroon: A Cross Sectional Survey in the Biyem-Assi Health District, Yaoundé." *BMC Women's Health* 16: 4.

Bodart, Claude, Gerard Servais, Yansane L. Mohamed, and Bergis Schmidt-Ehry. 2001. "The Influence of Health Sector Reform and External Assistance in Burkina Faso." *Health Policy and Planning* 16 (1): 74–86.

Brinkerhoff, Derick W. 1999. "State-Civil Society Networks for Policy Implementation in Developing Countries." *Review of Policy Research* 16 (1): 123–47.

Burkina Faso, Ministry of Health. n.d. "National Family Planning Stimulus Plan 2013–2015." http://ec2-54-210-230-186.compute-1.amazonaws.com/wp-content/uploads/2015/04/Burkina_Faso_National_FP_Plan_ENGLISH1.pdf.

Dodd, Mark, dir. *The Man Who Stopped the Desert*. June 2, 2010. www.imdb.com/title/tt1694580/.

Escobar, Arturo. 1995. *Encountering Development: The Making and Unmaking of the Third World*. Princeton, NJ: Princeton University Press.

Engberg-Pedersen, Lars. 2002. "The Limitations of Political Space in Burkina Faso: Local Organizations, Decentralization and Poverty Reduction." In *In the Name of the Poor: Contesting Political Space for Poverty Reduction*, edited by Neil Webster and Lars Engberg-Pedersen, 157–82. London: Zed Books.

Epstein, Helen. 2011. "Talking Their Way Out of a Population Crisis." *The New York Times*, October 22, 2011. www.nytimes.com/2011/10/23/opinion/sunday/talking-their-way-out-of-a-population-crisis.html.

Escobar, Arturo. 1995. *Encountering Development: The Making and Unmaking of the Third World*. Princeton, NJ: Princeton University Press.

Ferguson, James. 1994. *The Anti-Politics Machine: "Development," Depoliticization, and Bureaucratic Power in Lesotho*. Minneapolis: University of Minnesota Press.

———. 2006. *Global Shadows: Africa in the Neoliberal World Order*. Durham, NC: Duke University Press.

Gleick, Peter H. 2000. "A Look at Twenty-First Century Water Resources Development." *Water International* 25 (1): 127–38.

Goldman, Michael. 2006. *Imperial Nature: The World Bank and Struggles for Social Justice in the Age of Globalization*. New Haven: Yale University Press.

Haddad, Slim, Adrien Nougtara, and Pierre Fournier. 2006. "Learning from Health System Reforms: Lessons from Burkina Faso." *Tropical Medicine & International Health* 11 (12): 1889–97.

Harsch, Ernest. 2016. "Blowing the Same Trumpet? Pluralist Protest in Burkina Faso." *Social Movement Studies* 15 (2): 1–8.

Hawkesworth, M. E. 2012. *Political Worlds of Women: Activism, Advocacy, and Governance in the Twenty-First Century*. Boulder, CO: Westview Press.

Hickey, Sam. 2012. "Beyond 'Poverty Reduction through Good Governance': The New Political Economy of Development in Africa." *New Political Economy* 17 (5): 683–90. https://doi.org/10.1080/13563467.2012.732274.

Holt-Giménez, Eric, Annie Shattuck, Miguel Altieri, Hans Herren, and Steve Gliessman. 2012. "We Already Grow Enough Food for 10 Billion People . . . and Still Can't End Hunger." *Journal of Sustainable Agriculture* 36 (6): 595–98.

Kanji, Najmi. 1989. "Charging for Drugs in Africa: UNICEF'S 'Bamako Initiative.'" *Health Policy and Planning* 4 (2): 110–20.

Konadu-Agyemang, Kwadwo. 2000. "The Best of Times and the Worst of Times: Structural Adjustment Programs and Uneven Development in Africa: The Case ff Ghana." *The Professional Geographer* 52 (3): 469–83.

Lappe, Frances Moore, Joseph Collins, and Cary Fowler. 1981. *Food First: Beyond the Myth of Scarcity*. New York: Ballantine Books.

May, John F. 2016. "The Politics of Family Planning Policies and Programs in Sub-Saharan Africa." *Population and Development Review* 43 (51): 308–29.

Ministère de la Planification et du Développement Populaire. 1985. *Programme populaire de développement, octobre 1984-décembre 1985*. Ouagadougou, Burkina Faso: Imprimerie Nationale.

Ministère de la Santé. 2011. "Plan National de Developpement Sanitaire 2011–2020." Burkina Faso. www.uhc2030.org/fileadmin/uploads/ihp/Documents/Country_ Pages/Burkina_Faso/Burkina_Faso_National_Health_Strategy_2011-2020_ French.pdf.

Ministère de l'Economie et des Finances. 2000. "Cadre Strategique de Lutte Contre La Pauvreté. Burkina Faso." www. http://extwprlegs1.fao.org/docs/pdf/bkf147140.pdf.

———. 2011. "Burkina Faso SCADD: Stratégie de Croissance Accélérée et de Développement Durable 2011–2015." Ouagadougou, Burkina Faso. www.unpei. org/sites/default/files/e_library_documents/Burkina_Faso_PRSP_2011.pdf.

Murphy, Michelle. 2017. *The Economization of Life*. Durham: Duke University Press.

OECD. 2008. *Third High Level Forum on Aid Effectiveness: Accra Agenda for Action*. Paris: OECD Publishing.

———. 2011. *Aid Effectiveness 2005–10: Progress in Implementing the Paris Declaration*. Paris: OECD Publishing.

Organisation Mondiale de la Santé. 2009. "Stratégie de Coopération de L'OMS Avec Les Pays 2010–2015: Burkina Faso." Bureau régional de L'OMS pour l'Afrique.

Pande, A., A. Leive, M. Smitz, P. Eozenou, and E. Ozcelik. (2013). *Macro Fiscal Conext and Health Financing Fact Sheet*. Washington, DC: World Bank Aaka Pande; Patrick Eozenou; Adam Leive; Marc Smitz; Ece Ozcelik.

Pender, John. 2001. "From Structural Adjustment to Comprehensive Development Framework: Conditionality Transformed?" *Third World Quarterly* 22 (3): 397–411.

Reed, Julia. 2016. "Melinda Gates Focuses the World's Largest Foundation on Gender." *Wall Street Journal*, November 3, 2016. www.wsj.com/articles/melinda-gates-focuses-the-worlds-largest-foundation-on-gender-1478135700.

Ridde, Valéry. 2008. "'The Problem of the Worst-off is Dealt with after All Other Issues': The Equity and Health Policy Implementation Gap in Burkina Faso." *Social Science & Medicine* 66 (6): 1368–78.

———. 2011. "Is the Bamako Initiative Still Relevant for West African Health Systems?" *International Journal of Health Services* 41 (1): 175–84.

Sachs, Wolfgang, ed. 1992. *The Development Dictionary: A Guide to Knowledge as Power*. London and Atlantic Highlands, NJ: St. Martin's Press.

Sahn, David, and Rene Bernier. 1995. "Have Structural Adjustments Led to Health Sector Reform in Africa?" *Health Policy* 32 (1–3): 193–214.

Sangaré, Boubacar, and Gidéon Vink. 2015. "Une Révolution Africaine, Les Dix Jours qui Ont Fait Chuter Blaise Compaoré." Association Semfilms. www.film-documentaire.fr/4DACTION/w_fiche_film/46979_1.

Sankara, Thomas. 2007. *Thomas Sankara Speaks: The Burkina Faso Revolution 1983–1987*. 2nd ed. New York: Pathfinder Press.

Steinle, Aurora, and Denys Correll. 2008. *Can Aid Be Effective Without Civil Society? The Paris Declaration, the Accra Agenda for Action and Beyond*. Bronx, NY: International Council on Social Welfare (ICSW).

UNICEF. n.d. "The Bamako Initiative." www.unicef.org/sowc08/docs/sowc08_ panel_2_5.pdf.

Wolfensohn, James D., and Stanley Fischer. 2000. "The Comprehensive Development Framework (CDF) and Poverty Reduction Strategy Papers (PRSP): Joint

Note by James D. Wolfensohn and Stanley Fischer." www.imf.org/external/np/prsp/pdf/cdfprsp.pdf.

World Bank. 2011. "Burkina Faso: Overcoming the Odds." IDA at work. Washington, DC: World Bank Group. http://documents.worldbank.org/curated/en/163811468020359.

———. 2013. "Country Partnership Strategy for Burkina Faso for the Period FY13–16." Washington, DC: World Bank Group. http://documents.worldbank.org/curated/en/937251468005970222/Burkina-Faso-Country-partnership-strategy-for-the-period-FY2013-2016.

World Health Organization. 2011. "The Abuja Declaration: Ten Years On." www.who.int/healthsystems/publications/abuja_declaration/en/.

Wynter, Sylvia. 1996. "Is' Development' a Purely Empirical Concept or Also Teleological? A Perspective from' We the Underdeveloped'." In *The Prospects for Recovery and Sustainable Development in Africa*, edited by A.Y. Yansané, 299–316. Westport, CT: Greenwood Press.

3   Beggars can't be choosers

If we want to turn Africa into a new Europe . . . then let us leave the destiny of our countries to Europeans. They will know how to do it better than the most gifted among us.

– Ngũgĩ wa Thiong'o

If we take seriously the conditions that led the Kenyan writer and intellectual Ngũgĩ wa Thiong'o (2013) to entreat Africans to imagine a praxis tied to futures rooted in unique and particular African contexts, it becomes nothing short of compulsory to unpack the discursive aspects of ownership. Kenya, a former British colony located in East Africa, illustrates the pitfalls of accepting the ownership paradigm. Kenya has experienced a tumultuous political trajectory and volatile economic environment since independence in 1963. Politically, it has had only four post-independence presidents, two of whom were despotic by all accounts.[1] Economically, the country is exposed to exogenous shocks from the international market given its heavy dependence on primary commodity exports (Government of Kenya 1996). Members of the international community have linked the political and economic instability to low indicators of progress in Kenya's social sectors, especially health. International benchmarks for development show Kenya as lagging in its attainment of global health initiatives like the Millennium Development Goals (MDGs) and Abuja Declaration (United States Government 2014). The putative explanation for the country's besieged health sector is the Kenyan government itself. Although the range of actors influencing development extends beyond the Kenyan government, under the ownership paradigm the government assumes responsibility for the failed policies in the health sector. Kenya further illustrates how ownership absolves donors of responsibility for failed development while creating the space for donors to operate as an indispensable source of development expertise under the pretense of partnership.

I collected the data for this chapter during two trips to Kenya. During the first trip (in June of 2013) I spent four weeks in Nairobi interviewing policy-makers in the Kenyan Treasury (then known as the Ministry of Finance) and the Ministry of Education, along with academics at the University of Nairobi. My original intention was to focus this case study on Kenya's education sector. Working on the education sector became challenging when I realized that Kenya's major education program, the Kenyan Education Sector Support Programme (KESSP), had succumbed to a large corruption scandal in which billions of Kenyan shillings in donor funds went missing. In this context, posing questions about ownership (which is imbued with sentiments surrounding government-donor relations) proved difficult. Policy-makers in the Ministry of Education were apprehensive about discussing KESSP, and their responses to questions about ownership seemed tainted by their recent falling out with donors over the missing KESSP funds. During the first trip, the majority of my interviews were with government officials working in the external resource department of the Ministry of Finance who are responsible for working closely with specific donors operating in the various sectors in Kenya. This department also houses the office tasked with monitoring implementation of the Paris Declaration. Between government officials in the Treasury and the Ministry of Education and informants at the University of Nairobi, I collected twenty-five interviews.

During my second trip to Nairobi (from December 2015 through January 2016), I focused my data collection specifically on the health sector, conducting interviews with representatives of civil society organizations (CSOs) and donors working in Kenya's health sector. Within the Ministry of Health, I spoke with three top officials responsible for working with donors and developing the Kenya Health Sector Strategy. With respect to donors, I conducted semi-structured interviews with two officials at the World Bank, the Japanese International Cooperation Agency (JICA), and a former contractor with the European Union and the Danish International Development Agency (DANIDA). The number of interviews from this trip totaled twelve, bringing the overall total number of formal interviews in Kenya to thirty-seven.

During the interview process, I engaged respondents in elaborating the context within which they determine what ownership means to them. I also asked whether the government owns development in the health sector. To understand how ownership actually works in the Kenyan context, I triangulate three main sources of data: 1) my interviews; 2) government policy documents (such as the Kenya Health Sector Strategy, Kenya's Vision 2030, and the Medium-term Expenditure Framework); and 3) donor and civil society policy papers, e.g. the World Bank's country partnership for Kenya and the Health NGOs Network's strategic plan for 2014–2018 (HENNET

2014). I also draw on other primary sources such as Kenyan newspapers, along with secondary sources, including published reports on development in Kenya.

The next section outlines key economic and health policies in Kenya that reflect hegemonic development discourses and explores how they are rooted in the geopolitics of donor knowledge. The subsequent section answers the questions driving this research: What is ownership of development and how does it operate in Kenya? I find that Kenyan stakeholders view ownership according to their roles as defined under the ownership paradigm. Consequently, ownership leads to the same regressive outcomes in Kenya as in Burkina Faso. Ownership constructs donors as an indispensable source of development knowledge; however, donors do not share accountability with the Government of Kenya (GoK) for stagnant development in the country. As in Burkina Faso, the ownership paradigm reproduces the Kenyan development stakeholder as an undeveloped subject but through different means. In Kenya, the mistrust that characterizes donor-government relations continues a paternalistic relationship in which the government can never arrive at being an equal development partner with donors.

Investing in ownership: Taming the domestic

Kenya entered into the ownership paradigm under precarious economic conditions and a strained relationship with donors in 1999. Unlike many other African countries that adopted ownership in order to access Heavily Indebted Poor Country (HIPC) funds, Kenya was not eligible for HIPC (Thugge and Boote 1999; Hanmer et al. 2003). The World Bank and IMF did, however, require that Kenya produce a PRSP in order to continue receiving concessional lending from both institutions (Hanmer et al. 2003). The Bank and Fund recommenced giving concessional loans to Kenya in August of 2000, only to suspend them four months later in light of government corruption (Booth 2003). During this same period, the Kenya African National Union (KANU) government (Daniel Arap Moi's administration) was drafting their interim PRSP. The international financial institutions (IFIs) resumed lending, in 2002, to the new administration of Mwai Kibaki and the National Rainbow Coalition (NARC). The NARC government assumed power pledging to address corruption, implement economic reforms, and restore the government's relationship with the World Bank and IMF (Shiverenje 2005). Kibaki elaborated the Economic Recovery Strategy (ERS) predicated on the Bank and IMF's poverty reduction framework in 2002. While the final PRSP still awaited approval from the Bank and IMF, the NARC government drafted the Economic Recovery Strategy for Wealth and Employment Creation (ERSWEC), which set the groundwork for the

2004 approved version of the first iteration of the PRSP. ERSWEC, as a development strategy, focused on stimulating economic growth and economic recovery (Ministry of Planning and National Development 2003). Kenya's willingness to draft a Bank and IMF-approved poverty reduction strategy was the country's attempt to reposition itself within the larger aid architecture and demonstrate that the government was willing to play by the IFIs' rules on governance. For example, the second of the four pillars of the ERSWEC promotes "good governance," understood as being derived from the rule of law (Ministry of Planning and National Development 2003). Notably, the government's inability to create an environment conducive to good governance and rule of law were among the Bank and IMF's most enduring problems with the Kenyan government during the low-funding periods.

The Kenyan government continued to operate within the ownership paradigm when it produced the second iteration of its PRSP in 2008: Kenya Vision 2030. Slightly different from the goal of economic recovery, Kenya Vision 2030's ultimate goal is to turn the country into a middle-income country by the year 2030, ensuring that all of its citizens experience a "high quality life" (Ministry of State for Planning, National Development and Vision 2030 2008). The first Vision 2030 covered the period from 2008 through 2012. The second Vision 2030 covers from 2013 through 2017. Although the stated end goals may differ, both versions of the Vision 2030 carry forward the stated objectives in the ERSWEC, especially on the economic and political axes (Ministry of State for Planning, National Development and Vision 2030 2008).

Not only did the Kenyan government adopt these instruments, but the government stakeholders whom I interviewed also acknowledged their incorporation and elaboration as demonstrative of the government's commitment to development, often with a sense of pride. In fact, one World Bank official concurred that the GoK demonstrates ownership because it is "able to draw [its] own vision; they are able to translate that to medium-term plans and they follow through. These are the ingredients of ownership."[2]

In 1999, the Kenyan government implemented its first medium-term plan for the health sector: The National Health Sector Strategic Plan (NHSSP). NHSSP detailed the development goals and strategy for the health sector from 1999 through 2004. In line with the requirements of ownership, the government created NHSSP through a consultative process that extended beyond just the donor community. This strategic plan gave primacy to primary health care and to addressing the remaining constraints on health, thus indicating a desired shift from the previous neglect of the sector during the structural adjustment program era (Rono 2002; Mwabu 1995).

The second medium-term strategy, NHSSP II, spanned the following five years (2005 through 2010). NHSSP II (the first health strategy) incorporated more of the institutions under the ownership paradigm. In June 2006, the Joint Program of Work and Funding created the SWAp with significant donor support and with attempted (albeit limited) consultation involving other stakeholders in health (Glenngård and Maina 2007; Wamai 2009).

Participation and stakeholders

In accordance with ownership, when drafting the PRSP, countries must allow for a wide range of stakeholder participation, including members of civil society, parliament, and the private sector, as well as members of the donor community (OECD 2011). The underlying assumption is that wide participation from country stakeholders will increase the development strategy's staying power. Country stakeholders are also encouraged to aid in the implementation phase (OECD 2011). These actors, through various interventions, are responsible for implementing and maintaining the development strategy.

Kenya's PRSP has come under scrutiny for continuing to exclude the poorest populations from the consultation process, giving priority to expenditures that do not correspond with the poor's demands and failing to acknowledge the nuances of the poverty situation across the country (meaning that different social groups and regions experience poverty differently). The result has been to keep the final say for the PRSP in hands of technocrats at the ministerial level (Nyamboga et al. 2014; Calaguas and O'Connell 2002; Ufanisi 2002; Kiringai and Manda 2002; Wilks and Lefrançois 2002). Others have praised Kenya's PRSP as revolutionary and holistic, arguing that it has brought a refreshing element of participation and transparency to the policy formation process and, in many respects, helped align the strategy with community-level priorities (Hanmer et al. 2003; Shiverenje 2005; Swallow 2005). Despite these differences, few consider the exercise futile. Where the document is limited in its efficacy, there is a lack of political will or an inopportune political and economic environment (Shiverenje 2005; Hanmer et al. 2003).

In fact, much of the belief in Kenya's PRSP stems from the participatory element: The more participation in developing and implementing these poverty reduction strategies, the better the outcome for reducing poverty. Proponents of increased participation find this to be particularly true for the health sector (Olayo et al. 2014). Yet the focus on participation overlooks the uncomfortable reality that participation does not automatically translate into influence. Or, as one scholar states, "What began as a political issue is translated into a technical problem, which the development enterprise can accommodate with barely a falter in its stride. Incorporation, rather than exclusion, is often the best means of control" (White 1996, 7). In an attempt to indicate a shift to the ownership paradigm from the neoliberal development paradigm of the 1980s and 1990s, donors moved to bring the state and civil society back into the development process through increased participation. Accordingly, each of these stakeholders has a hand in the country's "owning" development. This also suggests that the limits of each stakeholder's participation are inscribed in the paradigm's principles.

One of the problems with the term "ownership" of development, however, is that its meaning and application are ambiguous (Buiter 2007). In the Kenyan context, there was more consensus across stakeholders regarding the definition of ownership. I found that the Kenyan government, civil society, and donors contributing to the Kenyan health sector all defined ownership in relative accordance with the conceptual definition given in the Paris Declaration and Accra versions of ownership: "Partner countries exercise effective leadership over their development policies and strategies and co-ordinate development actions" (OECD 2011, 3). Different from the dominant definition attached to the paradigm is the restricted view of ownership as being applicable only to the government. Distinct from donors and government officials, the Kenyan civil society representatives I interviewed saw their involvement in the process as central to bringing about ownership and development in Kenya.

Government

Despite being the dominant decision-making apparatus, government is not a monolithic entity; rather, it is a constellation of institutions, groups and ideologies. I thus interviewed a range of actors at the ministerial level. Despite there being considerable differences among the sectors and policy foci, those whom I interviewed in the Kenyan Treasury's External Resource Department and Ministry of Health (MoH) all had corresponding understandings of ownership: *Government* should be in charge of its policies, programs, and strategies. As a respondent in the External Resource Department put it, "We develop our own policy. We develop our own programs. We have our own strategies. And then, we tell our partners, this is the direction we are walking."[3] Or, more broadly, as an official in the MoH stated, "the country is in charge of its affairs."[4] Although the Paris document employs the term country with a range of government and nongovernment stakeholders in mind, and most of the Kenyan government respondents refer to the government as the agent responsible for ownership, the Paris document implies that government should be the leading stakeholder.

A number of respondents also used the metaphor of government being "in the driver's seat" to further explain ownership.[5] The government's rendering of ownership also places significant emphasis on donor support and presence in Kenya's overall development process. Referring to government and donors, one Ministry of Health official discussed the concept in these terms:

> Ownership of development ideally should be where we sit together and, of course, you are there to support me. We look at everything that we have. We agree on this, this is the direction . . . so this is what I have, you say what you have, and you support me to deliver on this.[6]

For Kenyan government respondents, there was very little mention of civil society being a necessary part of ownership. Donors seemed to be the primary partners in their quest for development through the ownership paradigm.

Donors

Under the ownership paradigm, donors should no longer be at the forefront of project and program implementation. In allowing government and country stakeholders to take more control of their development policies, donors should ease their grip on policy formation and implementation. All of the donors I interviewed made this abundantly clear: The national government (not donors) is responsible for implementation. Donors in Kenya should be providing technical expertise and building capacity at the government and local levels (UNDP 2009). The donor community in Kenya appears to have the same definition of ownership as the government and the OECD: "Country-led, country-initiated, country-driven and a process that actually addresses the concerns or the priorities of that particular government."[7] This was the general consensus among donors. Representatives I interviewed from key donor agencies argued that the country or government should determine its development trajectory. To the extent that donors are present, they should not impose their own agendas on the government. As with the Kenyan government's definition, there is no concrete mention of civil society. Ownership remains very government-centered. Civil society is not central to the ownership process from the donor perspective.

Much of this focus on government perhaps comes from the contentious relationship between government and donors. Kenya's history of limited implementation of donor conditionalities and what donors deem poor governance and corruption in the government continue to mar the donor-government relationship in Kenya. My interviews revealed a significant lack of trust between these two sets of development stakeholders. Both the World Bank and JICA identified implementation as one of the major challenges that they experience in working with government in the health sector. One Bank official gave the example of a health insurance subsidy program that is stalled in the government, which means that the Bank is "spending hours, and hours, and hours, chasing implementation instead of using the time to do other things."[8] As I will demonstrate later, this lack of trust between government and donors translates into the GoK begging for more "ownership" vis-à-vis donors.

Civil society

For key development stakeholders, understanding civil society's rendering of ownership is also essential. In Kenya, civil society organizations (comprising faith-based organizations, non-governmental organizations, and community-based organizations) began to receive development assistance directly in the late 1980s (Amutabi 2013).[9] Donors began to redirect funds from government projects and programs to NGOs in the late 1990s (Booth 2003). Within the ownership paradigm, CSO actors are responsible for a range of monitoring and implementation functions including

> to monitor the implementation of PRSP in the context of specific sectors and/or thematic groups, such as gender, governance, HIV/AIDS, pastoralism, natural resource utilization and management.
>
> (Shiverenje 2005, 29)

Each developmental sector has established an umbrella organization for CSOs operating within the particular sector. For health, the Health NGO Network – HENNET Kenya is the lead organization for the sector.

HENNET currently has ninety-two member organizations responsible for implementing health programs throughout the country. In addition to working in the realm of policy formation, advocacy and monitoring and evaluation of health programs, projects, and strategies, HENNET participated in elaborating the SWAp for Kenya's health sector (HENNET Secretariat 2014). The director of programing described the organization as being highly influential with respect to the health sector strategy: "In terms of the health sector strategic plan, I think we influenced a lot in terms of bringing on board [the] private sector and influencing health and contributing to health service delivery in the country."[10] As an organization, HENNET also receives a substantial amount of its financial support from bilateral donors. In fact, all the CSO representatives I interviewed were actively receiving donor funds. With HENNET, however, the contribution was notable: "I might say we are 50/50; HENNET depends majorly on donor funds."[11]

Not surprisingly, representatives from the civil society groups produced a more community-centered understanding of ownership. For example, one director of a NGO defined ownership as, "all actors participate in the entire cycle of development implementation and feel their decisions and contributions are valid and incorporated."[12] Another CSO respondent defined it in similar terms: "Feeling a part of the planning process [and] taking it as your own."[13] To give context to this definition, the respondent gave an example of ownership from her personal experience. Growing up in a part of Kenya where access to water was limited, she observed how donors would constantly come to her village and build water pumps without involving the community. When the pumps broke, members of the village community took no initiative to fix them. The village ultimately became littered with broken pumps. On one occasion, a donor organization came to build another pump; this time, however, they involved the community in the design and implementation stages of the project. While the rest of the pumps remain broken or have been removed, the NGO director noted how that particular pump remains a working fixture and reflects a sense of pride in the community. This example is representative of the general consensus on what ownership looks like in practice to people in civil society: The community being involved in the various stages of development projects and programs, a rendering of ownership that corresponds far more to the amendments made to the ownership paradigm at the Accra meeting. Interestingly enough, the CSO version of ownership does not have the same underlying sense of donor dependency as does the government version. In fact, one CSO respondent defined ownership as, "communities will think through innovative ways to deal when things continue beyond donor funding."[14]

Analyzing these three views on ownership illustrates the distinct manifestations of the concept on the ground, across the three main stakeholder groups. How people in each group engage the term is a matter of their position of power within their respective policy-making institutions. However, each of these stakeholders is aware of, and actively trying to increase ownership in, Kenya's health sector through the various stages of the policy-making process, from creation to monitoring and evaluation. The active pursuit of ownership on the part of each stakeholder demonstrates the level of investment each group has in the paradigm. What each group also understands is that the other groups are now permanent fixtures in the development process. As one Ministry of Health official put it, "[Donors] are now our partners, like the communities are our partners."[15] Again, this tripartite framework of government, donors, and civil society for development policy-making comes directly from the ownership paradigm. The paradigm does not, however, expose the ways in which donors shape preferences in the other two spheres.

How does ownership work in the Kenyan context?

Having subscribed to the ownership paradigm, Kenyan development stake-holders are now subject to the discourses that ownership produces. This section advances not with an attempt to measure ownership in Kenya, but with a description of discernible discursive themes that were manifest in my examination of the ownership paradigm in Kenya. I found that the paradigm solidifies donors as "development experts" who offer technical support and capacity building along with their financial services. As the development partners who contribute the expertise (and with aid flows to the country declining), donors are positioned to have a lasting role in Kenya's develop-ment process, making them an interminable part of the domestic policy-making process, and this has implications for ownership. According to the African Development Bank's president:

> Strengthening ownership is more difficult to achieve than it first appears, basically for two reasons. First, effective ownership requires that donors be willing to relinquish some control, and second, it requires that partner or recipient countries have demonstrable capacity to lead. Indeed, critical requirements for ownership are commitment to good governance and strong state capacity.
>
> (Kasekende 2006, 4).

Although donors have, and will continue to have, a lasting impact on devel-opment policies, Kenyan development stakeholders do not hold donors accountable when health policies fail to achieve their intended goals. This element – donors as an indispensable epistemic community of development experts with impunity – renders ownership in Kenya a chimera.

Donors as an epistemic community

The donor organizations that participated in this study all defined their role in Kenya's health sector as assisting the government through their analyti-cal abilities and technical expertise in ways that mirror consensual knowl-edge (Haas 1989, 1). With its promotion of measurable and evidence-based development strategies, the ownership paradigm facilitates the imposition of policies through consensual knowledge. The World Bank, for example, no longer imposes policies on the Kenyan government; it now exists to offer advice based on its research, which aids the government in carrying out policies. As one of the Bank officials I interviewed aptly noted, "When we present something, we present the evidence. We know that evidence is not everything in terms of policy, but we have strong evidence; you can persuade government to change its thinking."[16] This is the premise upon which an epistemic community operates – using evidence generated from "scientific" research to persuade governments to make policy decisions (Haas 2001; Haas 2015; Cross 2013). Another Bank official working in Kenya stated,

> Like I told you, we don't implement. What we do is advise, okay. We say, 'On the basis of the information available', because we do the analysis, 'this is what we recommend. These are the options.' And they choose their option. So, once they choose, we support them along whatever they have chosen that goes with our interest.[17]

What this statement indicates is how donors, through their analyses, limit the range of options available to governments. The Kenyan government, in turn, views donors in this way. In the official Kenyan Health Policy, the government outlines donors' role in carrying out the policy as follows:

> This policy recognizes that health services require significant financial and technical investment in a context of limited domestic resources. Donors and international non- governmental organizations have traditionally played a key role in providing resources for the health sector. This role has been structured around principles of Aid Effectiveness, which place emphasis on government ownership, alignment, harmonization, mutual accountability and managing for results of programs in the health sector.
>
> (Ministry of Health 2012, 31)

In practice, donors assume the role of knowledge experts and leave a lasting imprint on the episteme by designing the training of personnel working in the realm of particular diseases. For example, the respondent working with JICA explained, "one of our strong points is we do technical cooperation. Technical cooperation means we are able to bring some *expertise* that will [be] *embedded* in the ministry of health, provide policy advice, [and] provide strategic support."[18] In this way JICA becomes institutionalized in the Kenyan Ministry of Health. For example, JICA is in the process of implementing a new tuberculosis control program, part of which involves training personnel at the national level, along with providing laboratory equipment.

This degree of influence and determination of thought is permissible and reinforced through ownership due to the focus on measurable results and improved decision-making (Owa 2015; OECD 2011, 85).

The permanence and influence of donors as an epistemic community continues through the constant articulation of development in Kenya as being in a state of crisis. For example, the USAID's Country Development Cooperation Strategy for Kenya 2014–2018, states:

> The development context in Kenya is unstable and marked by numerous complex challenges. These include poor enabling environment for economic growth; half of the population living in poverty with limited access to basic services; chronic drought and food insecurity; stubbornly high maternal and under-five mortality rates; weak rule of law allowing corruption and a culture of impunity to flourish; natural resource degradation; increased radicalization; and a growing youth population with limited employment options putting pressure on social systems.
>
> (United States Government 2014, 3)

USAID maintains that it will aid in redressing these developmental lacunae by strengthening Kenya's ownership of its development strategy, which entails the relaying of "U.S. know-how, expertise and technology" (United States Government 2014, 92). Ultimately, the pervasive presence of donors in the health sector (and in development writ large) alludes to a permanent position for donors in the development process.

Donor longevity

By owning development, Kenya has committed to an interminable relationship with donors as development partners. Donors are so institutionalized in the various aspects of Kenya's development that parsing their influence at the level of policy-making can seem difficult. Within the National Treasury, there is now an Aid Effectiveness Secretariat responsible for tracking progress on the OECD's Aid Effectiveness forums. In Kenya's health sector, donors play a substantial role in funding HIV/AIDS, tuberculosis, and malarial service delivery. Donors generally fund between sixty and ninety percent of the health budget (Wamai 2009, 137). Thus, even though donor funding in Kenya's health sector is decreasing through the formal channels, donors continue to influence policy through informal channels. Close to one-third of Kenya's health expenditures are paid with donor funds and about 90 percent of that is off budget.[19] As mentioned previously, donor impact is not limited to government institutions but also manifested through the funding of many NGOs. With respect to HIV/AIDS, as one NGO director working in that sector explained, sixty percent of the policies for HIV/AIDS are donor-driven because seventy-five percent of HIV programs are donor-funded.[20] The general consensus among NGOs in the health sector is that if donors were to leave Kenya, the country would fall into a state of crisis. One NGO representative noted, "If a donor says they're closing shop today, you'd see a real crisis in Kenya."[21] Implementing Kenya's health sector strategic plan in two phases would cost the government 588 million Kshs in the first year and 344 million Kshs in the fifth year, and the government would still see a resource gap of 207 million Kshs after contributing 45 percent of the total cost (Ministry of Health 2014, 77). Although health investments increased from $17 US per capita to $40 US per capita from 1994 to 2010 (largely through government and donor contributions), Kenya's health sector is still deemed developing and under-funded.[22] In Kenya's revised PRSP for the IMF, the government lists as a targeted reform goal:

> Increase total government spending on health from the current 5.6 percent as a share of total public expenditure to 12 percent over the time period of this investment program. *Such an increase in the investments in human capital may seem ambitious, but past public spending per capita on health in Kenya has significantly lagged behind as compared to global and regional experiences.* In addition, the challenges described and the commitment of the government to make significant progress towards the Millennium Development Goals justify such an increase.
>
> (Government of Kenya 2005, 52; emphasis mine)

Kenya's commitment to MDGs and a number of other global health commitments forces the government to create "ambitious" policies that, if not achieved, will act as evidence for more donor interventions and cultivate a sense of underdevelopment.

Along with the financial dependency that will keep donors around is the language of partnership that surrounds ownership. A partnership implies a long-term relationship and Kenyan development stakeholders are invested in this language. During a conversation with a director in the Ministry of Education, I used the word "donors," and the director abruptly cut me off to let me know that they are no longer referred to as donors but, rather, development partners. In fact, in every interview, respondents consistently referred to donors as development partners. In reviewing the way in which donors defined ownership, Kenyans' reliance on donors is evident in their statements that ownership means that the government creates the policies in conjunction with donors, who then help by contributing much-needed resources. One policy official in the Ministry of Health remarked, "government ideally should lead agenda-setting, but there are limitations with resources and technical expertise."[23] Donors, according to the principles of ownership, necessarily overcome these limitations, as they are responsible for building country capacity. In joining the PRSP model, which also requires SWAps, donors are agreeing to help governments with their policy designs, development strategies, institutional reforms, and capacity building (Hill 2002). With this considerable amount of influence and the ubiquitous language of partnership, one would expect shared accountability across all development stakeholders. However, findings from my fieldwork suggest that the Kenyan government shoulders the responsibility for unsuccessful development.

Accountability

Ownership in Kenya entails government assuming sole responsibility for development outcomes, despite its partnership with donors. But since donors have been very present in designing development strategies, should they not also share responsibility for failed outcomes in the health sector? Although the language of ownership implies that both donors and government are to be held accountable, this is generally not the case.[24] I asked each respondent who was responsible when health policies failed to achieve their desired outcomes, and the overwhelming response was "the government." One government official's explanation suggests that accountability may differ, depending on the stakeholder. He opined,

> Normally government, generally, is held accountable as opposed to donors. But that is, strictly speaking, from an evaluative perspective. From the perspective of the population, of course, it is very different. [The population] will say, "well, the Germans, or the French, or whoever it was, came here and they left nothing." So, the population probably holds donors accountable for failures. A case in point, for instance, twenty, thirty years ago, there was a big water project in western Kenya, and they brought hand pumps which didn't work and which were not serviceable by the community. And they left them. Three years later, there was no water. The community does not blame the government; they blame the donors directly for that. Donors, of course, look at it very differently because they hold the government of Kenya accountable for failed policies, rightly or wrongly. In some instances, the local policies probably were not the best, or they were not backed by sufficient funding from the government side. But the flip side to that is that, also, the donor strategy was incorrect.[25]

On one hand, this account alludes to donors circumventing the government and going directly to the communities, which is problematic because it directly violates the ownership principles. But it also demonstrates the realpolitik of donor development practices. Donors are supposed to use government systems to deliver services because this reduces any duplication of effort, making aid more effective (Winters 2010). One interviewee articulated an ongoing battle that the GoK was having with the World Bank over the use of government systems:

> Currently, right now, there is a very huge fight with the World Bank because the World Bank is refusing to support devolution; and they want to support devolution using their own systems, which then makes it impossible to effectively deliver services that the Kenyans need. Then it means that when the projects are over, you'll again have to start setting up new systems. So, donors just need to stop and follow the country systems that have been set.[26]

If donors were, in fact, using government systems, communities would not be able to place the blame on donors, as the projects would appear to be coming from the government. On the other hand, with respect to accountability, the anecdote highlights the ways in which accountability between donors and government tends to be one-sided, with donors holding government accountable, but not the other way around. Furthermore, communities may hold donors responsible for projects because they design policies through input and influence tantamount to (and often greater than) the government's. The same respondent noted, however, that most Kenyans do not hold donors accountable "because they think [donor] funding is a great thing."[27] Donor funding being a "great thing" is reinforced by the development paradigm, in general, which is premised on donor funding being essential for sustainable progress. In this way, donors become reinforced as defenders of development.

Begging for ownership

The Kenyan government is very invested and complicit in reproducing the ownership principles. Take, for example, the government respondents' answers to my question about whether the government owns development or not. Perhaps more illustrative is the paradigm's ability to induce commitment to external interests. Officials in both the Ministry of Health and the Ministry of Finance strongly believed that the Kenyan government owns development, largely because the government has created its own national development policies and contributes the largest share of resources to development. In the Ministry of Finance, there was a strong sentiment that the GoK tells donors what to do and that, for the most part, they follow. Otherwise, it is the donors who impede ownership, not the government because the language of ownership gives government some leverage vis-à-vis donors. For example, one official in the Ministry of Finance expressed how "[donors] know that they have to take a back seat because, again, Paris, Accra, Busan is emphasizing the fact they are here to support."[28]

For many in the government, the ownership paradigm is supposed to mark a welcome shift in donor-government relations. Along with the requirement for increased participation, ownership should transform the relationship between government and donors from paternalism into partnership. Prior to Paris, respondents noted that although donors took the lead in development, their programs were scattered and did not use government systems. They implied, however, that not much has changed with respect to donor-government relations since the implementation of the Paris agreement. There remains a dearth of trust between donors and the Kenyan government. More specifically, donors' belief in the Kenyan government's commitment to development continues to wane.

Partnership or paternalism?

Because of Kenya's weak performance in implementing structural adjustment policies, the IMF and World Bank suspended lending to the government a number of times. Several of these suspensions took place during the Daniel Arap Moi and KANU administration (Booth 2003; Shiverenje 2005). In 1997, the IMF deferred loans under the enhanced structural adjustment facility because of poor governance on the Moi administration's part. During this period, the government had to borrow at market rates, which negatively affected an already deteriorating economy (Devarajan, Dollar, and Holmgren 2001). In order to resume borrowing from the IMF in 1996, the GoK had to complete a series of structural reforms, including reduction of the civil service sector and privatization of forty public businesses by the end of that year (Camdessus 2000, 714). According to the IMF, the GoK made a decent start but never implemented the full range of reforms, leading the IMF to refuse lending until the it made substantive adjustments (Camdessus 2000). In the face of IMF and Bank claims that the government did not fully implement reforms, others have noted that, in 1997, the Kenyan government executed the swiftest round of deregulation of any African country.[29] This strained relationship has not completely dissipated. In fact, there remain lingering trust issues between donors and government, impacting the degree to which donors can see the GoK as committed to development.

Despite the elaboration of the PRSP and incorporation of the concomitant instruments and institutions, donors continue to view the government as lacking ownership of development. In the health sector, donors refuse to offer budget support – a modality for disbursing aid funds at the government's discretion. Donor funds in health circumvent the government completely, either going directly to NGOs or to specific health programs. Consequently, donors restrict the government's ability to redirect funds to the issue areas that it deems important (Wamai 2009). The Swedish International Development Agency (SIDA), a bilateral donor in Kenya's health sector, explained the situation as follows, "Kenyan donors are faced with the contradiction of attempting to convey ownership in the absence of partnership. Low donor trust of the Kenyan government's commitment to transparency and openness in budgetary matters implies that dialogue with the government is prevented from making progress on ownership issues" (Weeks et al. 2002, iii). In this same report, SIDA argues that Kenya is lacking ownership because it does not commit to and take responsibility for its development activities (Weeks et al. 2002). The rest of the donor community in Kenya appears to share these sentiments.

In 2009, donors and the GoK began participating in the Development Partnership Forum Meetings (DPF) and the Pre-Development Partnership Forum Meetings. These meetings bring together the various donors or development partners and top Kenyan government officials to establish different commitments for the GoK to achieve by the next meeting. The DPFs are institutional manifestations of the ownership paradigm: These fora operate in the context of strengthening the partnership between the government and donors in order to facilitate more government ownership. The title of these meetings, however, is very misleading. A review of the notes and transcripts from the 2010 Pre-DPF, 2010 DPF, 2012 DPF and the 2013 DPF, reveals that these meetings appear to be forums for donors to assess the GoK's progress towards meeting its development commitments (Government of Kenya 2010, 2011, 2012, 2013). The World Bank representative, Johannes Zutt, on the other hand, represented donors with more peremptory remarks, alluding to a less-than-equal partnership. What one finds in these forums is not the GoK telling donors what to do or donors eagerly awaiting the government's command on the next step forward.

Despite rhetoric suggesting equally valid input from governments and community partners with regards to development strategies, donors' preferences have become more entrenched and pervasive, while their conditionalities percolate deeper into government operations beyond the realm of development. During the meetings mentioned above, the World Bank representative, Zutt, used language regarding the GoK's progress on their agreed upon obligations that suggested the desire for greater commitment from government. He stated, "For our partnership to work best, we need to trust that agreeing to these commitments will also result in getting them done, expecting unforeseen circumstances. It is a matter of mutual credibility and accountability" (Government of Kenya 2012, n.p.). He, furthermore, suggested that "Kenya is living beyond its means" and must do more to promote growth and reduce poverty (Government of Kenya 2012, n.p.). In line with ownership, Zutt chided the government for its poor governance record and the potential consequences that might arise if this persisted. He argued that donors are "ambassadors" for other sources of foreign aid, but this means nothing if Kenya does not create "business-friendly" policies and ensure that "corruption does not impede equal competitiveness" (Government of Kenya 2012, n.p.). Zutt continued,

> Many donors will shape their future aid program in the light of their assessment of Kenya's governance – how well the government manages the election process, its planning and budgetary processes, its macroeconomic levers, the fight against corruption, and the agenda for structural reforms.
>
> (Government of Kenya 2012, n.p.)

If nothing else, this statement demonstrates the conveniently capacious conceptualization of governance that inexorably links donors to entities in the Kenyan government – all under the auspices of development.

These forums also illustrate donors' extensive involvement in monitoring the GoK, especially in light of the history between both stakeholders. Donors interviewed during my fieldwork in Kenya corroborated these accounts with respect to the health sector. One of the Bank officials whom I interviewed stated,

> I would say, for Kenya, we don't have a problem in terms of capacity of government to actually implement. What I see is a lack of commitment from the government to implement. For example, in the health insurance subsidy program, which is being implemented through the national hospital insurance fund, it doesn't matter what type of support you give them, things just don't move. Uh, I think it's a typical civil servant's way of working, which derails the process.[30]

Donors do not reserve their mistrust just for the Kenyan government. Representatives whom I interviewed from local CSOs also voiced frustration with donors who withhold funds because they do not trust the NGO.

> [Donors] are after their money, but you, you are after your development. So, you see the two contrast [sic]. You want to build a school,

but the donor's telling you, give me the accountability. . . . You know, accountability works before you start your work. The first form you receive is how are you going to account for the money. There's no trust.[31]

As the respondent noted, the dollar is the bottom line for donors. And the larger paradigmatic orientation towards increased effectiveness measured through tangible results exacerbates these types of interactions. For example, the Paris Declaration makes clear the need to improve aid effectiveness in the face of growing doubt from constituents in donor countries regarding the utility of foreign aid (OECD 2011). Ironically, perhaps, the language of ownership, has the unintentional consequence of providing the Kenyan government some space for agency.

Government respondents place the responsibility for blocking ownership on donors. Several respondents argued that donors make it difficult to implement the Paris Declaration. Although they believed that Kenya was better off than it had been prior to Paris, a number of donors still refuse to let Kenyans take the lead in their development trajectory. According to the ownership principles, donors are supposed to work within government's framework for development. As I argued previously, many of these donors had been essential in developing these frameworks, yet a number of them refuse to work within the guidelines. One of the major culprits is the United States Agency for International Development (USAID). A Ministry of Health official explained that almost all of USAID's funding is off-budget, meaning that it is not delivered through the GoK but instead through third parties,[32] namely civil society organizations that also work with the government to implement development strategies. When donors go straight to CSOs, however, they are not using government systems. One Kenyan who worked with two different donor organizations expressed how this approach damages the government:

I think even donors are to blame in this country because there is a tendency for donors here thinking that they can drive this system. Well, indeed, they have not been able to do that. And, one of the problems is that the donors have been able to infiltrate and penetrate the government and make it ineffective, replacing government funding with the project funding that doesn't last for long.[33]

The principles of harmonization and alignment give Kenyan NGOs and government the rhetorical leverage to make these claims. Previously, during structural adjustments, there was no formal agreement between African stakeholders and donors indicating the need for donors to use African systems. Still, there remains little room within the ownership architecture for

Kenyan stakeholders to operate outside of donor influences. One of the ways African governments, the GoK included, have been able to gain leverage vis-à-vis donors that is not predicated on the formal language of ownership is by not implementing certain policies (Whitfield 2009; Van de Walle and Ndulo 2014). Thus, where donors see the Kenyan government as untrustworthy and lacking ownership, the government is actually employing one of the few tools it has to counter donor hegemony over development. It embraces overtly the rhetoric of ownership while covertly subverting the very same.

The mistrust that undergirds the relationship between donors and the Kenyan government illuminates the circumscribed possibilities for any type of truly Kenyan-derived approach to development under the ownership paradigm. Through its adoption of ownership, the Kenyan government subscribes to the pervasiveness of donors through institutions like the DPF under the guise of partnership. The logic informing the ownership paradigm facilitates this paternalistic interaction in which the GoK must defer to donor knowledge and authority over all development matters, underscoring further that ownership does not require donors to release *all* control, but only *some* control. With ownership's emphasis on governments having capacity and demonstrating good governance, when these conditions are not met, donors can justify not relinquishing control. In this light, the relationship between donors and the Kenyan government, based on the dynamics of the ownership paradigm, can legitimately remain paternalistic. To the extent that the Kenyan government can only show its displeasure with policy direction by not implementing said policies, one must ask: How truly useful is this version of ownership in allowing aid-recipients to articulate their development vision vis-à-vis donors?

Conclusion

Both theoretically and practically, ownership does not operate to give Kenyan stakeholders more control over the direction and substance of their health development policies vis-à-vis donors (OECD 2011, 29). Under the terms of the ownership paradigm, the Ministry of Health and Ministry of Finance and Economics should not only design and implement health policies, they should also be able to coordinate all other actors involved (OECD 2011). Civil society actors in the health sector should be able to participate in the policy development and implementation processes so that health outcomes reflect the needs of civil society and the poorest segments of the population. By aligning their financial support with these health policies and using national systems and institutions to deliver this support, donors could, in turn, create a space for more local ownership.

Following the tenets of ownership should lead to increased aid effectiveness, which would lead to more tangible results in the health sector. These results would mean reducing national poverty. Accountability for these development outcomes would fall on both donors and Kenyan stakeholders' shoulders (Owa 2015).

Ownership does not necessarily function in such a fashion that the Kenyan government designs and controls the road map of development. In examining health and economic policies in Kenya, the mechanisms through which ownership emerges become all the more salient. Critically, I find a rhetorical shift in development practices since the Paris Declaration, not a substantive change. Yet, the rhetoric is not without consequences. In Kenya, ownership places responsibility for health sector outcomes in the government's hands, absolving donors of significant responsibility for poor development results. The language embedded in the ownership paradigm also turns donors into an epistemic community; their role is to provide knowledge and expertise to the Kenyan government. What follows, then, are permanent institutions for donors within the Kenyan government, like the Development Partnership Forums and Aid Effectiveness Secretariat. Consequently, donor presence becomes an indispensable part of Kenya's health and economic sectors.

Notwithstanding the CSO director's praise for the donor organization that built a pump and incorporated members of the village in the planning and implementation process, the donors came to the village already knowing that they were going to build a pump. The community had little say in that part. Thus, the consultation with the village, making them feel as if they had a substantial input, was misleading. If the villagers could have said, "we don't want a pump, we want a school," this would have shown that the villagers were in charge of identifying their own needs. But the donor group came in with an agenda (to build a pump) and succeeded in making members of the community believe that they had made a significant contribution. Ownership offers a false sense of choice, which one Bank official acknowledged: "We say, on the basis of the information available, because we do the analysis, this is what we recommend, these are the options, and they choose their options."[34] What such statements overlook are the ways in which the information and analysis that donors provide as experts reflect a provincial set of knowledge about development. Nevertheless, the ownership paradigm propagates this provincial set of knowledge as universal and objective. The information and analyses that donors like the World Bank offer constitute and reproduce power differentials across development stakeholders in ways that must be questioned if Kenyan stakeholders are to envision and implement a form of development that conforms to their unique context.

Notes

1 Jomo Kenyatta, Kenya's first president, ruled through a one-party system and died in office. After his death, Daniel Arap Moi assumed power without holding elections and remained in power, ruling with an iron fist, until the first multi-party elections in 2002. In 2007, the country erupted in civil unrest during the second national election for the Kenyan presidency. Violence broke out between supporters of the two dominant rivals, Mwai Kibaki and Raila Odinga.

2 0051Donor, 05/01/2016_Nairobi, Kenya.

3 JM0626, 26/06/2013_Nairobi, Kenya.

4 0047MoH, 02/01/2016_Nairobi, Kenya.

5 DK0618, 18/06/2013_Nairobi, Kenya, HM0618, 18/06/2013_Nairobi, Kenya, MA0620, 20/06/2013_Nairobi, Kenya, KY0619, 19/06/2013_Nairobi, Kenya.

6 0049MoH, 04/01/2016_Nairobi, Kenya.

7 0051Donor, 05/01/2016_Nairobi, Kenya.

8 0052Donor, 01/08/2016_Nairobi, Kenya.

9 Civil society in Kenya comprises non-state actors. HENNET refers to itself and member organizations as the private sector in their strategic plan, which is not odd in Kenya since, according to one NGO director, there are times when the private sector is included under the civil society umbrella (0053CSO, 01/08/2016_Nairobi).

10 0053CSO, 08/01/2016_Nairobi, Kenya.

11 Ibid.

12 0057CSO, 15/01/2016_Nairobi, Kenya.

13 0056CSO, 15/01/2016_Nairobi, Kenya.

14 0053CSO, 08/01/2016_Nairobi, Kenya.

15 0047MoH, 02/01/2016_Nairobi, Kenya.

16 0052Donor, 08/01/2016_Nairobi, Kenya.

17 0051Donor, 05/01/2016_Nairobi, Kenya.

18 0050Donor, 05/01/2016_Nairobi, Kenya.

19 0052Donor, 08/01/2016_Nairobi, Kenya.

20 0056CSO, 15/01/2016_Nairobi, Kenya.

21 Ibid.

22 Nyamboga et al. (2014) argue that there is a gap across policies, institutions, and poverty reduction strategies in Kenya. Even though the government has increased spending on development and poverty reduction, poverty rates in Kenya remain high.

23 0049MoH, 04/01/2016_Nairobi, Kenya.

24 The Paris Declaration states that the declaration was "developed in a spirit of mutual accountability," (2008,3). This is also one of the partnership commitments, which translates to both government and donor stakeholders taking responsibility and holding each other accountable while being transparent.

25 AA0626, 26/06/2013_Nairobi, Kenya.

26 0054Donor, 08/01/2016_Nairobi, Kenya.

27 Ibid.

28 KY0619, 19/06/2013_Nairobi, Kenya.

29 In his account of structural adjustments while conducting fieldwork in Kenya in 1997, James Howard Smith notes that Kenya was "plunged into darkness" as the government began the heavy round of neoliberal adjustments coming from the IMF and World Bank (2008,35).

30 0052Donor, 08/01/2016_Nairobi, Kenya.
31 0058CSO, 15/01/2016_Nairobi, Kenya.
32 0049MoH, 04/01/2016_Nairobi, Kenya.
33 0054CSO, 08/01/2016_Nairobi, Kenya.
34 0051Donor, 05/01/2016_Nairobi, Kenya.

References

Amutabi, Maurice N. 2013. *The NGO Factor in Africa: The Case of Arrested Development in Kenya*. New York: Routledge.

Booth, David, ed. 2003. *Fighting Poverty in Africa: Are PRSPs Making a Difference?* London: Overseas Development Institute.

Buiter, Willem. 2007. "Country Ownership, A Term Whose Time Has Gone." *Development in Practice* 17 (4–5): 647–52.

Calaguas, B., and M. O'Connell. 2002. "Poverty Reduction Strategy Papers and Water: Failing the Poor?" Water Aid Discussion Paper, www.partnershipsforwater. net/psp/tc/TC_Tools/002F_PRSP%20failing%20poor.pdf, Accessed Feb. 9, 2016

Camdessus, Michel. 2000. "Looking to the Future: The IMF in Africa." http://cit eseerx.ist.psu.edu/viewdoc/download? doi=10.1.1.692.5560&rep=rep1&type=pdf.

Cross, Mai'a K. Davis. 2013. "Rethinking Epistemic Communities Twenty Years Later." *Review of International Studies* 39, (1): 137–60.

Devarajan, Shantayanan, David R. Dollar, and Torgny Holmgren. 2001. *Aid and Reform in Africa: Lessons from Ten Case Studies*. Washington, DC: World Bank Publications.

Glenngård, Anna H., and Thomas M. Maina. 2007. "Reversing the Trend of Weak Policy Implementation in the Kenyan Health Sector? A Study of Budget Allocation and Spending of Health Resources versus Set Priorities." *Health Research Policy and Systems* 5: 3.

Government of Kenya. 1996. *Economic Reforms for 1996–1998: The Policy Framework Paper*. Nairobi: Government of the Republic of Kenya.

———. 2005. *Kenya: Revised Poverty Reduction Strategy Paper*. Washington, DC: International Monetary Fund.

———. 2010. *Third Development Partnership Forum*. Nairobi, Kenya: Aid Effectiveness Kenya.

———. 2011. *Pre-Development Partnership Forum*. Nairobi, Kenya: Aid Effectiveness Kenya.

———. 2012. *Fourth Development Partnership Forum*. Nairobi, Kenya: Aid Effectiveness Kenya.

———. 2013. *5th Development Partnership Forum (DPF)*. Nairobi, Kenya: Aid Effectiveness Kenya.

Haas, Peter M. 1989. "Do Regimes Matter? Epistemic Communities and Mediterranean Pollution Control." *International Organization* 43 (3): 377–403.

———. 2001. "Policy Knowledge: Epistemic Communities." In *International Encyclopedia of the Social and Behavioral Sciences*, edited by N. J. Smelser and B. Baltes, 17–11578. Cambridge: Cambridge University Press.

———. 2015. *Epistemic Communities, Constructivism, and International Environmental Politics*. London: Routledge.

Hanmer, Lucia, Ikiara Gerrishon, Walter Eberlei, and Carolyn Abong. 2003. "Kenya." In *Fighting Poverty in Africa: Are PRSPs Making a Difference?* edited by David Booth, 91 – – 119. London: Overseas Development Institute.

HENNET Secretariat. 2014. *HENNET: Health NGO Network Strategic Plan 2014–2018: As a Network We Strengthen Civil Society's Engagement & Contribution to the Health Sector*. Nairobi, Kenya: Health NGO Network.

Hill, Peter S. 2002. "The Rhetoric of Sector-Wide Approaches for Health Development." *Social Science & Medicine* 54 (11): 1725–37.

Kasekende, Louis. 2006. "Country Ownership of Policy Reforms and Aid Effectiveness: The Challenge of Enhancing the Policy Space for Developing Countries in Aid Relationships." Statement presented at the Aid as Negotiation: Workshop, Oxford, September 26.

Kiringai, Jane, and D. Manda. 2002. "The PRSP Process in Kenya." Paper Presented at the Second Meeting of the African Learning Group on the Poverty Reduction Strategy, Brussels, 18–21 November. pdfs.semanticscholar.org/177a/480dec0bc3c9122f8e0c531c4b11dc3ee324.pdf?_ga=2.231330589.343143324.1556292022–153770752.15562920

Ministry of Health. 2012. *Kenya Health Policy 2012–2030*. Nairobi, Kenya: Government of the Republic of Kenya.

———. 2014. *Kenya Health Sector Strategic and Investment Plan (KHSSP)*. Nairobi, Kenya: Government of the Republic of Kenya.

Ministry of Planning and National Development. 2003. *Kenya: Economic Recovery Strategy for Wealth and Employment Creation 2003–2007*. Nairobi, Kenya: Government of Kenya.

Ministry of State for Planning, National Development and Vision 2030. 2008. *First Medium Term Plan (2008–2012): Kenya Vision 2030: A Globally Competitive and Prosperous Kenya*. Nairobi, Kenya: Government of the Republic of Kenya.

Mwabu, Germano. 1995. "Health Sector Reform in Developing Countries: Making Health Development Sustainable Health Care Reform in Kenya: A Review of the Process." *Health Policy* 32 (1): 245–55.

Nyamboga, Tom, Benson Nyamweya, Adam Sisia, and Gongera George. 2014. "The Effectiveness of Poverty Reduction Efforts in Keya: An Evaluation of Kenyan Government's Policy Initiatives on Poverty Alleviation." *International Affairs and Global Strategy* 23. www.iiste.org/Journals/index.php/IAGS/article/view/14175.

OECD. 2011. *Aid Effectiveness 2005–10: Progress in Implementing the Paris Declaration*. OECD Publishing.

Olayo, Rose, Charles Wafula, Evalyne Aseyo, Constantine Loum, and Dan Kaseje. 2014. "A Quasi-Experimental Assessment of the Effectiveness of the Community Health Strategy on Health Outcomes in Kenya." *BMC Health Services Research* 14 (1): 1–13.

Owa, Masumi. 2015. "Is OECD DAC's Aid Effectiveness Agenda Based on Evidence?" *Journal of Development Effectiveness* 7 (4): 435–44.

Rono, Joseph Kipkemboi. 2002. "The Impact of Structural Adjustment Programmes on Kenyan Society." *Journal of Social Development in Africa* 17 (1): 81–98.

Shiverenje, Hudson. 2005. "What Happened to the PRSP in Kenya? The Role of Politics." *PLA Notes* 51: 27–31.

Smith, James Howard. 2008. *Bewitching Development: Witchcraft and the Reinvention of Development in Neoliberal Kenya*. Chicago: University of Chicago Press.

Swallow, Brent. 2005. "Potential for Poverty Reduction Strategies to Address Community Priorities: Case Study of Kenya." *World Development* 33 (2): 301–21.

Thiong'o, Ngũgĩ wa. 2013. *In the Name of the Mother: Reflections on Writers and Empire*. Kenya: Boydell & Brewer Ltd.

Thugge, Kamau, and Anthony R. Boote. 1999. *Debt Relief for Low-Income Countries: The Enhanced HIPC Initiative*. Washington, DC: International Monetary Fund.

United Nations Development Programme (UNDP). 2009. "Capacity Development: A UNDP Primer." www.undp.org/content/undp/en/home/librarypage/capacity-building/capacity-development-a-undp-primer.html.

United States Government. 2014. *Kenya: Country Development Cooperation Strategy: 2014–18: Sustainably Transforming Kenya's Governance and Economy*. Washington, DC: United States Agency for International Development.

Van de Walle, Nicolas, and Muna Ndulo. 2014. *Problems, Promises, and Paradoxes of Aid: Africa's Experience*. Newcastle upon Tyne: Cambridge Scholars Publishing.

Wamai, Richard. 2009. "The Kenya Health System – Analysis of the Situation and Enduring Challenges." *Japan Medical Association Journal* 52 (2): 134–40.

Weeks, John, David Andersson, Chris Cramer, Geda Alemayehu, Hailu Degol, Frank Muhereza, Matteo Rizzi, Eric Ronge, and Howard Stein. 2002. "Supporting Ownership: Swedish Development Cooperation with Kenya, Tanzania, and Uganda." Sida Evaluation 02/33:1. www.oecd.org/countranzaniaania/35203817.pdf.

White, Sarah C. 1996. "Depoliticising Development: The Uses and Abuses of Participation." *Development in Practice* 6 (1): 6–15.

Whitfield, Lindsay, ed. 2009. *The Politics of Aid: African Strategies for Dealing with Donors*. New York: Oxford University Press.

Wilks, A., and F. Lefrançois. 2002. *Blinding with Science or Encouraging Debate? How World Bank Analysis Determines PRSP Policies*. London: Bretton Wood Project and World Vision. www.brettonwoodsproject.org/topic/adjustment/a30blinding.html.

Winters, Matthew. 2010. "Accountability, Participation, and Foreign Aid Effectiveness." *International Studies Review* 12: 618–43.

4   Ownership in comparison

What the new paradigm seems to be principally about is getting African
governments to accept, implement, and legitimate policies made in Europe
and North America largely in the interests of Western banks.

                                                               – James Ferguson

The empirical chapters in this book highlight the ways in which ownership
of development is defined and implemented in two African countries. Burkina Faso and Kenya represent different geographical, historical, cultural,
political, and economic contexts. Despite these differences, the discursive practices embedded in the ownership paradigm produce very similar development strategies. My analysis of development policy evolution
in the health sector of both countries reveals how the paradigm leads to
more donor-dependency and cultivates a sense of underdevelopment, while
absolving donors of any responsibility for failed development outcomes in
Burkina Faso and Kenya.

Consolidating the discourse

Ferguson's (2006) observation speaks to the ways in which the ownership
paradigm necessitates consolidation of certain discursive practices in order
to maintain traditional power dynamics across donors and African governments. Ownership of development as the guiding discourse for improving
aid effectiveness and achieving development outcomes in aid-receiving
Africa is pervasive across both Burkina Faso and Kenya. The Paris Declaration on Aid Effectiveness provides the consolidated definition, and
subsequently hegemonic version, of ownership: "Partner countries exercise effective leadership over their development policies, and strategies,
and co-ordinate development actions" (OECD 2011, 29). Since the signing
of the Paris Declaration in 2005, a range of development stakeholders has

leveraged the concept for varied and sometimes conflicting ends (de Renzio, Whitfield, and Bergamaschi 2008; Buiter 2007). Although scholars and policy makers attribute the ownership concept to the OECD high-levelfora, this has always not been the case. Earlier in this book, I situated the origins of *ownership* in the World Bank and IMF's need to re-legitimize their existence as necessary engines of development in debt-ridden and impoverished countries (Pender 2001; Owusu 2006).

For the World Bank, the process of re-legitimization entailed elaborating a set of rules of engagement for development different from those used during the formal structural adjustment era. The resulting comprehensive development framework is an articulation of what the Bank's superficially changed engagement would look like: Long-term and comprehensive development strategies; countries owning their reforms by "devising and directing" their own development agendas; partnership between development stakeholders (primarily government, donors, civil society, and the private sector); and performance based on measurable results (Wolfensohn and Fischer 2000; Wolfensohn 2005). These rules of engagement form part of the set of instruments, measures, discourses, and practices commensurate with the ownership paradigm. Incorporated in the paradigm is the usage of Sector Wide Approaches (SWAps), Poverty Reduction Strategy Papers (PRSPs), and Medium-Term Expenditure Frameworks (MTEFs) as the standard policy tools for development, and the principles of ownership, partnership, poverty reduction, while the dominant actors are donors, the state, and civil society. There are also international institutions that inform domestic-level development goals, such as the Millennium Development Goals (MDGs) and, now, the Sustainable Development Goals (SDGs).

Much like the PRSPs, identification of legitimate stakeholders, and focus on poverty reduction, SWAps and MTEFs are products of the World Bank. Local actors in Burkina Faso and Kenya have also adopted the language of partnership and ownership. In both countries, one finds a version of development consistent with the ownership paradigm. Both countries possess a PRSP that is tied to a SWAp for the health sector through a MTEF. Burkina Faso has the Vision 2020 as its long-term development strategy and Kenya has its Vision 2030. These two strategies give primacy to rapid economic growth as key to poverty reduction, along with other factors like good governance and foreign direct investment (Ministry of State for Planning, National Development and Vision 2030 2008; Ministère de l'Economie et des Finances 2011).

Donors in both countries no longer carry the formal title of "donors." In accordance with the Paris Declaration and Accra Agenda for Action (AAA), they are now development partners (Paris Declaration 2012). Burkinabe and Kenyan stakeholders have fully adopted this change in nomenclature.

For Burkinabe, donors are now *les partenaires technique et financier* (PTF), or technical and financial partners. Kenyans refer to these same actors as development partners. Although all development stakeholders should be partners, based on the consensus coming from the AAA, in Kenya, the term partner is reserved specifically, if informally, for donors. To gauge the extent to which local actors had internalized this change in rhetoric, I formulated my interview questions in both countries using the term "donor," making sure to use "development partner" only after the respondent referred to donors in this way.

Chapter three demonstrates how committed the Kenyan government (GOK) is to the notion of partnership, as it seemingly provides leverage for the government when negotiating with donors over development policies. Government officials in Burkina Faso, while they did employ the language of partnership in conversation, were not as committed to it. Burkinabe civil society proved different. During a conversation with a friend who worked with one of the local associations responsible for carrying out national health programs, I kept referring to *les donateurs*. This friend at least waited until the end of the conversation to tell me that they were no longer referred to as donors, but as *les PTF*. In practice, however, Burkinabe actors continued to use *les PTF* and *les bailleurs de fond* interchangeably.[1] At the official level, both countries have consolidated the language of ownership, and development policies and frameworks unequivocally refer to donors as partners. In Kenya, the government has truly bought into the partnership rhetoric. Informal interactions with informants in both countries revealed a difference between Burkina Faso and Kenya that results from their country-specific renderings of ownership, which itself is a function of their historical engagement with aid and development.

By formally consolidating the language of ownership, both countries attain the same outcomes with respect to donors and development. In Burkina Faso and Kenya, whether referred to as donors, PTF, partners, or *bailleurs de fond*, local stakeholders have codified donors as sources of development "knowledge." Although the development industry has always implied this relationship between African countries and aid-giving countries, owning ownership, as it were, cements this asymmetrical dynamic (Alemazung 2010; Keita 2011).

Even the informal measures of ownership persist across both cases. Donors in Burkina Faso's health sector measure the degree to which the government owns development according to its ability to finance the associated programs and projects. As one donor at the United Nations Population Fund (UNFPA) in Ouagadougou stated,

Je crois que, oui, [le gouvernement s'approprie le développement] parce que, quand on regardait déjà le niveau de ressource domestique

que le pays injecte, c'est qu'à même importante. (I believe so, [the government owns development] because when having looked at the level of domestic resources that the government injects, that is at least important.)[2]

The same thought process is evident across Kenyan civil society organizations (CSOs), as the following quote from a Nairobi-based NGO representative illustrates:

I don't think there is ownership; and if there is ownership, then the political will is not there because the key factors, like I've already told you, 75 percent of HIV [treatment and prevention activity] is donor funded. . . . I think the highest we've allocated to health in the national budget was about 7 percent.[3]

Although the OECD measurement for ownership makes no mention of who should fund development policies, stakeholders on the ground are suggesting that this should be the government's responsibility. The OECD's formal measure for ownership is meant to account for context-specificity. What the informal practices show is a more standard measure that clashes with the particulars of each country. For governments themselves, being able to fund the development programs and projects that correspond with international targets for progress trivializes the degree to which those same governments are attempting to design their own development trajectories in accordance with their available resources. Ultimately, interpreting ability to fund development as a measure of ownership reinforces the assumptions of universality embedded in the current paradigm, as is evident in the various health commitments and targets to which the Kenyan and Burkinabe governments must agree. The implicit universality is consistent with the funding-gaps that both governments encounter in trying to attain these targets.[4]

Scientific capitalism: The mediating discourse

One evening in July, at the World Bank headquarters in Ouagadougou, I sat in the shared work office transcribing interviews I had collected that day. To my right was an economist whom the Bank had contracted for a short-term project on governance and, to my left, an American student pursuing his Master's in Political Science at Yale. We were all typing feverishly when a Burkinabe IT specialist working for the Bank walked in. He asked whether we were economists, to which he received one yes and two noes. He then asked why, with all these economists here (meaning in the World Bank) hasn't the country seen any progress? Coming from a permanent employee of the World Bank, this seemed perhaps to be part of some well-known institutional joke to which I was obviously not privy. So, I responded by asking, "Isn't the country experiencing an eight percent growth in GDP?" "*Ah, bon?*" he said. "Are we really, because there is a difference between real growth and GDP growth." Now, he had my full attention. Maybe the problem isn't growth, but how the growth is shared, I said. He nodded and added,

> That's true, you need both. But after SAPs, which didn't work (*des chaos*, to be exact), we've still had nothing but economists with their models, paradigms, and formula that don't work. We say the Minister of Finance must be an economist. Basically, all government officials must be economists. Even here, at the Bank, everyone is an economist, but their recommendations haven't yet produced progress. I think the whole discipline needs to change.

I waited for him to finish with a laugh that would indicate how uncommitted he was to his previous statement or some indication that he was joking. I listened in vain. Instead, hoping to get more from the gentleman, I said, "It is, in fact. There are changes happening within the discipline." In an honest and telling manner, he responded, "I just think we need other people with different trainings and backgrounds making decisions."[5]

This vignette from my field experience in Burkina Faso is emblematic of the hegemonic influence of economics in African development. Mkandawire states,

> the economics profession in Africa has rarely been critical of its epistemological foundations, nor has it seriously considered the deontology of the profession, especially the implications of its material underpinnings and social construction on the integrity and credibility of its research.
>
> (Mkandawire 2014, 173)

Donors like the World Bank, IMF, and USAID produce and offer this knowledge set as a scientifically sound and value-neutral approach and, consequently, understanding of development (Ferguson 2006). This scientific capitalism is part and parcel with the ownership paradigm, contributing to the construction of donors as knowledge experts on development because of their "technical" and economic acumen.

Donors operate as part of an epistemic community that offers insulated policy input based on a purported "expertise" that they bring to development in Burkina Faso and Kenya by way of their mastery of economics. The overall purpose of an epistemic community is to change state interests through the application of consensual knowledge, which functions best during periods of uncertainty or crisis (Haas 1989). In the health sectors of both countries, the epistemic community of donors provides the governments with "advice" regarding sound policies for strengthening the respective health sectors, policies that are always somehow rooted in the market. The World Bank, the World Health Organization (WHO), USAID, and other donors produce policy papers and publications about the conditions of country-level and global health with the intention of offering policy advice. The production of policy papers alone does not make these donor organizations epistemic communities in health. It is the other factors, such as their institutionalization around consensual knowledge and the perpetual crisis in the health sectors, that facilitate this process.

I mentioned previously that the ownership framework is predicated on donor involvement in development. Donors' role in development, and in the health sector more specifically, is to equip governments with the technical capacity to deal with the technical problems that accompany establishing a fully functioning health system. Donors also provide financial assistance that can translate into consumable health commodities, such as workshops and trainings that build and strengthen capacities. Using the word "technical," however, presumes a certain level of objectivity surrounding the donor contribution to development. On the ground, technical is imbued with normative implications around knowledge. As one donor working with JICA in Kenya noted, "One of [JICA's] strong points is we do technical cooperation. Technical cooperation means we are able to bring in some expertise that will embed in the Ministry of Health provide policy advice, provide strategic support."[6] This same arrangement exists in Burkina Faso with the United Nations Development Programme (UNDP), leading one of their officials to say,

> Ce qu'on entend par le renforcement de capacité, en d'autre terme, c'est vraiment les accompagner pour que eux même ils puissant avoir le compétence pour assurer les actions de développement qu'ils auraient définir. (What we mean by capacity building, in other words, it's really accompanying them so that they themselves can have the competence to secure the development actions that they would define.)[7]

That JICA is a bilateral donor and UNDP multilateral demonstrates how this view of donor responsibility and superiority in development knowledge vis-à-vis the Kenyan and Burkinabe governments is not a question of multilateral versus bilateral politics. Instead, it is a question of whether donors conform to their roles as indicated in the Paris Declaration and Accra Agenda for Action.

The Paris Declaration identifies capacity building and "strengthening partner countries' national development strategies and associated operational frameworks" as part of donor responsibilities in carrying out the plan for aid effectiveness and increasing partner countries' abilities to actually own development (OECD 2011; OECD 2008). The explicit role of donors as knowledge experts is also evident in the original Comprehensive Development Framework (CDF). Former World Bank president James Wolfensohn, in propagating the Bank's new framework, made clear that the Bank would act as "a source of knowledge" and no longer "implement" projects. This framework reinforces the *consensual knowledge* that protects donors from government criticism. It also explains why there is a false distinction between technical expertise and policy advice. Policy advice assumes that there are other viable alternatives; technical expertise assumes an inarguable truth with respect to a given problem. The consensual knowledge that binds donors to technical expertise plays out in the design of strategies and solutions to development problems, problems that are often the consequence of the strategy itself.

Attempting to change government interest and consensual knowledge is necessary but not sufficient for explaining the ways in which the ownership paradigm reproduces donors as an epistemic community. There must also be a state of crisis or uncertainty. The ownership paradigm presents the interminable crises around poverty and underdevelopment in order to further validate the epistemic community of donors. One of the ways in which epistemic communities maintain power in a given policy arena is through the contribution of technical expertise during periods of crisis. Generally, the technical knowledge that the community contributes is deemed too complicated for political officials to ascertain on their own (Haas 1989). The need for ownership and its associated procedures grows directly from the crisis around global poverty and the twin challenges of meeting the UN Millennium Development Goals while improving aid effectiveness. The World Bank has been instrumental in creating this fear. The creator of the CDF and ownership paradigm, former Bank president James Wolfensohn, articulated his vision of CDF in a speech titled "The Other Crisis." He states,

> In response to the current crisis, we at the Bank have been focusing on putting in place the short- and the long-term measures for sustained recovery. Working with governments on financial, judicial, and regulatory reform, on bankruptcy laws, anti-corruption programs, and corporate governance – so essential to the restoration of private sector confidence. Before the crisis hit, we had already worked on financial sector reform in sixty-eight countries. At the request of our

shareholders, we have now expanded that capacity by one-third, and we are reinforcing our leadership in corporate governance.

(Wolfensohn 1998, 4)

Wolfensohn is referring to the crisis of global poverty – a world in which millions of people go without food, health care, education, etc. He and others central to the epistemic development community deem these problems to be the consequence of poor economics internal to each country. Take, for example, the World Bank's assessment of Burkina Faso's social and economic standing with respect to implementation of the country's first PRSP:

> Burkina Faso is faced with daunting economic and social problems, from the slow process of privatization and private sector growth to below-benchmark social indicators. However, if the country continues to improve its economic management and sustains its commitment to poverty reduction, there is a good probability that it can implement the PRSPS and, in the process, make solid progress toward achieving the Millennium Development Goals, a parallel target of the government
>
> (World Bank 2003, 25)

By suggesting that the problem is rooted in economics, it follows that, so too, is the solution. The problem that the IT specialist at the World Bank articulated is pervasive and part and parcel with the maintenance of donors as "development experts." Instead of viewing the knowledge generated within the communities of economists as being a set of internally derived and maintained opinions about development, both governments accept the policy advice coming from donors as rooted in sound, empirically-tested evidence. Thus, when the Kenyan government, which accepts the ownership paradigm, refuses to implement donor-backed policies, this is an affront to science and evidence-based development. Similarly, when rural Burkinabe women choose to abstain from modern contraceptives, it is not a matter of personal choice but an indication of backwardness and blatant rejection of development. Atomizing responsibility for structural problems aids in the exoneration of donors for failed development outcomes.

Impunity with influence

The ownership paradigm and accompanying global targets around health give donors as an epistemic community considerable input in the policy-making decisions and development designs in Burkina Faso and Kenya, but they do not lead to more donor accountability. The Paris Declaration makes clear the considerable engagement that donors will have in increasing aid effectiveness in aid-dependent countries and helping these countries reduce poverty and achieve the MDG targets. As an epistemic community operating with the agreed-upon goal of fostering development, donors have embedded themselves within the policy-making processes in Burkina Faso and Kenya.

Beyond just direct government-donor negotiations over policy preferences, bilateral and multilateral donors also reinforce their influence through global agendas and within civil societies at the local level. Ownership facilitates this process, as the OECD states that ownership grows out of the need to better integrate international initiatives into domestic-level policymaking (OECD 2011). Both Burkina Faso and Kenya have incorporated the numerous global health initiatives into their health sector strategies. The top four most influential are Global Fund to Fight AIDS, Malaria, and Tuberculosis; Global Alliance for Vaccines and Immunizations (GAVI); President's Emergency Plan for AIDS Relief (PEPFAR); and the World Bank Multi-County AIDS Programme (MAP). These large funding sources shift the priorities of health workers from other health concerns to target these globally recognized diseases (Ravindran 2014). The MDGs also inform the health development strategies in Kenya and Burkina Faso. As I have indicated previously, both countries use MDGs as one of the major guidelines for determining success in their health sectors.

In being considered partners, which implies shared responsibility, donors participate in a number of policy decisions in both countries. The health sector policies and strategies in Burkina Faso and Kenya are demonstrative of the partnership that characterizes the government-donor relationship during the policy-making process. Both governments, however, look differently at the ways in which donors go about exercising their partnership. In Kenya, the government officials I interviewed suggested that they only support what the government wants. Burkinabe policy-makers described their role as an *accompagnement* (accompaniment). While the Kenyan government officials held fast to the notion that donors merely support the government through technical and financial assistance, Kenyan civil society organizations operating in the health sector thought differently. Respondents whom I interviewed from various civil society organizations stated that health policy was donor-driven, especially with respect to HIV/AIDS. According to respondents, donors drove the health sector proportionate to the financing they contributed. One director noted, "If a donor says they're closing shop today, you'd see a real crisis in Kenya and a real crisis in any African country. Because I think, in terms of donor-dependency, it's not just a Kenyan thing, it's across [Africa]."[8] This is not unlike the statement that the employee in the local association in Burkina Faso made regarding health associations' loss of funding: Loss of donor funding is nothing to laugh about.[9]

When the call for ownership was formalized at the OECD, so too was the accompanying framework for delivering the long-term, holistic, development approach that is integral to demonstrating a country's ownership. The Bank's role in designing these instruments translated into their responsibility for approving the first generation of PRSPs. Prior to either country being able to access the Heavily Indebted Poor Countries (HIPC) funds, the World Bank and IMF had to approve both Burkina Faso and Kenya's development strategies. This fact never figured into any of my respondents' rationales for why and how donors influence development in the respective countries. A World Bank official in Nairobi brought up the question of ownership very early in our conversation. I later asked whether he thought that there could be genuine "ownership" if the World Bank and IMF had to approve the plans? He quickly retorted, "No, they don't have to be approved." I followed up by saying "originally," to which he gave a rapid, "yeah, originally, but now they don't."[10] The emphasis was on how these institutions no longer "impose" their beliefs. I continued to push: "Right, because [countries] are now able to do it by themselves." Exasperated, he responded, "They simply share. Yeah, they do it through a consultative process; it is a requirement, which they have to do. So [countries] go and do it themselves in a consultative process and then share with us. We don't endorse or whatever."[11] This level of influence rarely factors into how power relations between donors and governments is observed. Donor respondents focused more on the observable forms of influence like funding.

Financially, donors have considerable influence in the health sectors, consistent with their role as capacity builders and ownership enforcers. However, finance as a form of influence is becoming less salient in Kenya. In Kenya, thirty-eight percent of the development budget came from external development partners in 2014/2015, a reduction of nineteen percent from the 2013/2014 fiscal year (National Treasury 2014), but health expenditures also declined. Donors contributed close to twenty-six percent of the total health expenditure in 2012/2013, down from thirty-five percent in 2009/2010 (Ministry of Health 2012). With respect to reproductive health, which included family planning, donor contributions fell from twenty-two percent in 2009/2010 to eighteen percent in 2013 (ibid.). These estimates do not include the considerable funding that donors allocated to development projects through NGOs and civil society organizations.

Donor ability and desire to circumvent government and directly target community-level associations speaks to another element of influence donors wield over development strategies and outcomes. One of the more persistent problems that representatives of governments in Burkina Faso and Kenya brought up in interviews was donors reallocating funding to NGO and civil society projects. This was the case especially in the health sector, where there are many NGOs willing to deliver health services like contraception and medications. Both governments expressed discontent with this process. One policy-maker in the Burkinabe Ministry of Health recounted,

> Les PTF, ils vont directement au niveau communautaire même. Ils sont en train d'aller ver là-bas parce qu'il y a, on a trop politique, quoi. Ça veut dire, on parle plus qu'on réagisse. Au niveau communautaire, quand on va directement, c'est l'action même. Donc eux, ils préfèrent aller directement [au niveau communautaire]. Ils sautent plus des étapes. (The donors go directly to the community level. They go there directly because [the government] is too political. That means we talk more than we do. At the community level, it's about action. So [the donors prefer] to go directly to the community. They're skipping steps.)[12]

But as the policymaker noted, "Ça aussi, ce n'est pas une très bonne chose, parce que nous [le gouvernement], on a un plan qui est là, qu'il faut suivre." (That's also not a very good thing, because we [the government] have a plan in place that we must follow.)[13] In Kenya, government officials expressed the same frustrations: "Most of [USAID] funding doesn't run through the budget. Most of the, almost all of it, is kind of off-budget. So, they work through third parties."[14] One of the respondents at USAID agreed, stating, "It's hard for governments to tell donors how to spend their money."[15]

These accounts of donors, especially USAID, circumventing government control and instead interacting directly with communities and NGOs demonstrate the multiple axes of intervention that donors have within development. As noted in Chapters two and three, every civil society organization in this study stated that they either could not function without donor funding or would have a very difficult time doing so. If donors are circumventing government to carry out different development projects, what does that mean for the governments' abilities to lead and direct all development stakeholders?

Through international commitments, designing government strategies, and funding local NGOs donors are influencing health policies in these two aid-dependent African countries. Despite their evident influence at various levels, the dominant narrative remains that donors do not influence health policies, which means that they cannot be held accountable if those policies produce undesirable outcomes. Responding to the question, "Who is held responsible when health policies do not produce the desired outcomes?" the resounding answer across both countries and with multiple stakeholders was the government, not governments and donors. My interviews revealed how development stakeholders in Burkina Faso and Kenya view the respective governments and not donors as responsible for policy outcomes; this view is not inconsistent with the hegemonic language of ownership since country ownership purports to put governments – not donors – in control of development.

Feeling underdeveloped

As Gustavo Esteva (1996) aptly observes, "For two-thirds of the people on earth. . . 'development' is a reminder of *what they are not*" (1996, 10; emphasis in the original). Chapters two and three have illustrated how the ownership paradigm reproduces through different means Burkinabe and Kenyan stakeholders' perceptions of self as underdeveloped. Consistently attributing failed policies to national stakeholders in both countries reinforces the notion that their development problems are internal to their respective countries and not a consequence of historical and structural inequalities. In accordance with the dominant rationale for Africa's underdevelopment, the new culprit is its institutions (Grovogui 2001). Neither country can develop due to its cultural institutions and mores, such as family planning systems, or state-level institutions that are not conducive to good governance. Burkinabe development stakeholders also referred to themselves and their nation as being underdeveloped, often in the context of not having enough resources to meet their development objectives. Coincidentally, this frame of thinking justified donor presence in Burkina Faso. Viewing themselves as underdeveloped and in need of donor help to develop was manifest in Burkina Faso's family planning policies and the implementation of these policies at the community level. In Kenya, ownership reproduced the underdeveloped subject through a continual rejection of the Kenyan government as a legitimate partner in development.

In Burkina Faso, the paradigm constructs as underdeveloped the Burkinabe man and woman who abstain from family planning methods deemed legitimate under the neoliberal model of development. As I demonstrated in Chapter two, local associations in Tenkodogo receive funding from the *Programme d'Appui au Développement Sanitaire* (PADS) to carry out a range of health-related activities aimed at implementing the national and sector-wide strategies for the health sector. Along with the Burkinabe government, donors such as the World Bank, GAVI Vaccination, and the UNDP list and fund specific health objectives that local associations are expected to carry out in their communities. One of the dominant objectives is to teach men and women with the intention of changing their attitudes and behavior (*sensibiliser* in French) about the benefits of family planning methods like modern contraception and the spacing of births. Such teaching implies changing an individual or community's behavior through the delivery of relevant, evidence-based information. Acting in a manner that does not conform to the behavior-modifying information indicates backwards thinking and a "traditional" mindset. By interviewing respondents from these health associations, I was able to see how the health workers employed these modernizing and underdevelopment discourses to persuade men and women in Tenkodogo to adopt this rendering of family planning. Not divorced from the international discourses around family planning in Africa, the health workers intimated that women and men who refused to use modern contraception and space out their births were keeping the country from meeting the MDGs or putting an undue burden on the population. As I demonstrated in Chapter two, by demarcating the line between what is women's empowerment and what is not, family planning policies under the ownership paradigm dis-empower women, making them view family structures that do not conform to the nuclear model as backward and traditional.

Underdevelopment in Kenya, at the state-level, happens through a different process. The Kenyan government attempts to mobilize the development discourse and adopt the associated practices as demonstrative of their equal status with donors and commitment to development. Fredrick Cooper explains,

> Development ideology was originally supposed to sustain empire, not facilitate the transfer of power. Yet developmentalist arguments – about labor and policy as much as economic planning – were something trade union and political leaders in Africa could engage with, appropriate, and turn back. This framework allowed them to pose demands in forms that could be understood in London or Paris, that could not be dismissed as 'primitive'. . . . Much as one can read the universalism of development discourse as a form of European particularism imposed abroad, it could also be read . . . as a rejection of the fundamental premises of colonial rule, a firm assertion of people of all races to participate in global politics and lay claim to a globally defined standard of living.
> (1997, 84).

Even before the advent of the ownership paradigm, Kenya was appropriating the language and practice of hegemonic development. As I mentioned previously, Kenya was the first African country to accept structural adjustment packages from the World Bank and IMF. It was also the first African country to adopt a family planning program that promoted women using some form of contraception, at a time when other African leaders were skeptical of the Malthusian logic embedded in the push for population control policies (Obadina 2014). The Kenyan government has also been long open to a market approach to development, even when its neighbors were experimenting with economic socialism as a model for development (Okereke and Agupusi 2015). Consequently, it is not surprising that the GoK has taken up the ownership paradigm as its own.

Chapter three laid out how the Kenyan government fully adopted the ownership discourse by using the associated development tools, i.e. SWAps, MTEFs, and PRSPs, and consulting civil society and other non-state stakeholders regarding policy options to address the country's development problems. The government even established an aid effectiveness secretariat. Government respondents have also appropriated the ownership discourse and demonstrate that they have mastered the development lexis, referring to donors only as their partners and invoking the Paris Declaration and Accra Agenda for Action (AAA) as illustrative of a shift in donor-government power dynamics. Prior to elaborating its first PRSP, the Kenyan government even used these same principles of long-term development strategies for poverty reduction with broad stakeholder participation to produce its National Poverty Eradication Plan (NPEP). However, the World Bank and IMF did not consider NPEP a legitimate poverty reduction strategy (Hanmer et al. 2003). Still, despite the GoK's numerous attempts to demonstrate its commitment to the ownership paradigm, donors operating in the country do not trust it and suggest that the government lacks ownership (Weeks et al. 2002; United States Government 2014). Donors' inability to trust the Kenyan government (and at times civil society) was a dominant theme emanating from my fieldwork in Kenya. Much of the donor distrust is rooted in the GoK failing to implement agreed-upon development policies and programs.

Refusing to implement agreed-upon programs and policies is an example of the GoK exercising some agency with respect to the country's development (Whitfield 2009). However, such actions by the government are not deemed legitimate under the ownership paradigm. For example, the putative definition of ownership only accounts for government implementing and taking responsibility for development (OECD 2011). Thus, in failing to implement policies or take responsibility for them, the GoK cannot "own" development according to these discursive restraints. Nevertheless, because the Kenyan government attempts to show that it has mastered the required development lexis, adopted the modes of sanctioned communication with the Development Partnership Forums, and met the other requirements for genuine partnership with donors, the donor community continues to engage the GoK in a paternalistic relationship. Donors I interviewed consistently lamented the constant monitoring and pursuit of implementation that they felt was necessary vis-à-vis the GoK. And because the paradigm constructs donors as the development experts, not to implement their recommended policies suggests that the GoK is acting in bad faith and rendering Kenya perpetually underdeveloped.

When Kenyan and Burkinabe development stakeholders choose actions that do not conform to the principles, science, or solutions that donors deem to be valid to produce development, the current development paradigm reproduces the stakeholder as underdeveloped. The examples of family planning in Burkina Faso and policy implementation (or governance) in Kenya illustrate the ways in which the ownership paradigm cultivates a sense of underdevelopment under the pretense that the government cannot make development decisions without the "expertise" that donors provide. Acting in their capacity as "development experts" and working towards measurable indicators of aid's effectiveness, donors present African stakeholders with what seem to be their only options for development. In turn, the purveyors of the ownership paradigm attempt to keep local stakeholders reliant on western knowledge for indications of progress. It is, however, only an attempt. Although one of the implicit goals of the ownership paradigm is to de-politicize development, remnants of politics are trapped in the different country renderings of ownership.

Footsteps versus revolution: Politics matter

In Kenya, government and civil society-based stakeholders produce a rendering of ownership informed by the World Bank and OECD's definition, that is, they accept the hegemonic definition of ownership. For these actors, ownership refers to the state and community's ability to control its development trajectory vis-à-vis donors. The notions of ownership in Burkina Faso veer drastically from the OECD and Bank's definition and, consequently, from the Kenyan rendering. Burkinabe stakeholders view *l'appropriation de developpement*, ownership of development, as a particular level of consciousness regarding the individual's role vis-à-vis the community in bringing about development. Much of the difference between the Burkinabe and Kenyan conceptualizations comes from the way in which the countries initially engaged the neoliberal paradigm. The introduction of SAPs in Burkina Faso and Kenya marked a critical moment for reifying the ontological possibilities for development in both countries. The legacies of this crucial juncture are not always evident at the level of path-dependent policies in both countries (Thelen 1999; Pierson 1993), but instead at the ideational level.

In both Burkina Faso and Kenya, executive institutions left lasting legacies with respect to stakeholder engagement with development. Notably, Kenya was the first African country to receive a structural adjustment loan in the 1980s. Then-President Daniel Arap Moi was quite open to the economic

changes that the World Bank and IMF required as conditions for the stabili-
zation package that the country required during its second economic reces-
sion. A generally welcoming disposition towards donors was characteristic
of the Moi regime. Although he kept a tight grasp on the political processes
in the country, Moi's economic policies were commensurate with the neoliberal development framework coming from the international financial
institutions (Smith 2008; Maathai 2008). His *nyayo* (footsteps) development proposed an incremental approach to progress (Smith 2008). As Kenyans suffered from budgetary cuts to the social sectors, *nyayo* development
sought to elicit a consensus for patience from the population waiting to reap
the benefits of these policies (Moi 1986). While Moi was in Kenya pushing
nyayo, for a brief period in the 1980s Thomas Sankara was attempting to
revolutionize Burkina Faso in a direction opposite that of structural adjustments. During the mid- to late-1980s, Thomas Sankara, whom some have
called the last African revolutionary, came to power in Burkina Faso. To
understand local renderings of ownership, one must take into consideration
the politics and legacy of Thomas Sankara. Sankara came to power in 1983
by overthrowing a military government with the help of the military and
civilians (Harper-Shipman 2018). Although he was also a military officer,
he included civilians prominently within the ranks of the National Council for the Revolution (CNR) government (Harsch 2013). While he was in
power and since his assassination in 1987, Sankara's approach to development has offered an alternative to the current neoliberal and ownership
models of development prevailing in Burkina Faso.

Thomas Sankara's development model borrowed heavily from the ideologies of socialism and Marxism, leading him to promote a national identity
based on self-reliance and social solidarity and, with these, an anti-charity
sentiment across the social and political sectors (Sankara 1985; Martin
1987). This is not to suggest that the country was not receiving external aid during this period. Rather, aid from international donors targeted
projects only (Harsch 2013; Wilkins 1989). This very targeted aid was a
consequence of both Sankara's development philosophies and dominant
donor opposition to these same philosophies. For example, once France,
the United States, the World Bank, and other major international donors at
the time became aware of Sankara's anti-charity, anti-debt, anti-structural
adjustments, and anti-neo-imperialist politics, they became anti-Thomas
Sankara, and France and the World Bank ceased offering budgetary support
to the Burkinabe government during Sankara's tenure (Gabas, Faure, and
Sindzingre 1997). Where donors did remain present, the Sankara government created a consultation table that required them to sit down and work
with the Burkinabe government around his new model of development
(Harsch 2013; Zagré 1994).

A staunch anti-neoliberal, Sankara refused to accept the neoliberal structural adjustment packages that the World Bank and IMF were demanding of other indebted nations throughout the 1980s. His position found fertile ground among Burkinabe, as I learned in speaking with an older Burkinabe man about the political uprisings of the early 2000s. He began to talk about his time in the military under Sankara. More specifically, he recounted how opposed Sankara was to structural adjustment policies. The man recalled that during one of his speeches to the military, Sankara told the soldiers never to accept the structural adjustment packages that the World Bank and IMF were imposing across the rest of the continent. He insisted that accepting SAPS would be akin to selling out your family so that only a few members could eat. Instead, he advocated for a collective tightening of belts. Everyone, he proposed, should tighten their belts until the period of economic hardship had passed because if the country accepted the SAPs, it could never pull out. As we spoke, the old man went on to lament how Burkina Faso sits today exactly where Sankara predicted it would. When former president Blaise Compaoré took office after Sankara's death, one of the first things he did was implement World Bank and IMF structural adjustment policy reforms.[16]

In unpacking this the older gentleman's narrative, one dominant theme of Sankara's development approach is evident: The country must develop using the resources at its disposal. In asking that Burkinabe make do with the country's available resources, Sankara was imposing a different type of adjustment program, distinct from the one that spread hardship across all groups (Savadogo and Wetta 1991). In relying primarily on domestic resources, the government was still able to spend more on the health and other social sectors than in previous years (Harsch 2013). Although the country was experiencing challenging economic conditions during this time period, the Sankara government was still able to make noticeable changes in the public health sector. By 1986, the government built 7,460 primary health posts (almost one per village) throughout the country (Harsch 2014). Public health spending also increased by twenty-seven percent between 1983 and 1987 (Savadogo and Wetta 1991, 60). Furthermore, 2.5 million children received vaccinations (Smith 2015). During this same period, Moi was implementing structural adjustments in the health sector that led to increased infant mortality rates, a decline in doctor-to-population ratios, and an increase in overall poverty rates (Muga et al. 2005; Rono 2002).

Sankara's self-reliance model meant that the national economy would operate based on domestic interests. The needs of subsistence farmers and rural communities would take precedence over exports that served international interests (Zagré 1994). The government departed from a top-down approach in allocating resources and focused instead on the needs of people and institutions at the grassroots level. To this end, the government relied on social mobilization and community self-help projects to promote development. These community self-help projects were essential to maintaining the Sankara model of development during periods of economic hardship (from 1983 to 1984, in particular). Alternatively, *nyayo* reinforced a notion that development can only come from the state; Kenyans could not obtain development without fierce loyalty to the state (Smith 2008).

Along with sharing hardship across the different groups, Sankara's model of adjustment also pushed Burkinabe to buy locally. In another conversation, a young man not yet born during Sankara's time in office invoked the leader's revolutionary spirit to explain the history of imperialism in Burkina Faso. This young man related how Sankara once said that the African was so busy trying to fight the imperialists, but Africans should look down at their plates: Imperialism was sitting on their plates as they consumed rice and other imported foods from Western countries, despite producing these same foods in their own countries.[17] Stories like this serve the dual purpose of illustrating Sankara's impactful legacy, as well as the alternative path of development that Burkina Faso was undertaking during his short time in office.

The different histories of commitment to neoliberal development largely inform the disparate conceptualizations of ownership between Burkina Faso and Kenya. Kenya was initially open to the types of reforms and development that came with structural adjustments in the 1980s and 1990s. The Moi regime implemented many of these economic policies and even began allowing symbolic multiparty elections, in 1992, in response to international pressure (Smith 2008; Brown 2001; Devarajan, Dollar, and Holmgren 2001). In this way, the continuation of neoliberal policies through PRSPs is commensurate with the history of Kenyan government policies. Ownership in Kenya looks like "being in control of policies" with no inherent contradiction because the country has long been oriented towards market-driven policies. The genesis of this thinking can be seen in the *African Socialism* doctrine of Jomo Kenyatta. Kenyans have, thus, had a long and sustained engagement with the market-driven form of development, and the consequences are evident in their commitment to the ownership paradigm. Because Kenya has long been oriented toward a market approach to development, Kenyan stakeholders have adopted perspectives of ownership that conform to market-based descriptions of their respective roles. Representatives from the Kenyan government overwhelmingly defined ownership in terms of the government taking the lead in drafting development plans with donor support. Alternatively, civil society representatives defined the ownership as the process whereby all members of society are included in the development planning process. The ownership paradigm, which remains grounded in neoliberal development discourse, clearly defines the state's role as "taking the lead" in drafting and implementing development policies through a partnership with donors, while civil society exists to be consulted and serve as watch-dogs of government implementation.

Sankara's model of development called for a type of ownership arising from Burkinabe society, making it ontologically different from the version of ownership that donors and IFIs created and continue to proffer. Ownership under the Burkinabe alternative meant individual sacrifice for collective progress along with a deep-rooted, autochthonous understanding of the individual's position and responsibilities within the collective to further development. Sacrifice pertained to the need to thrive with the resources available in the country and to forgo the Faustian-bargain that came with the development that the West was promoting through SAPs and foreign aid. Sankara's spirit remains embedded in Burkinabe notions of ownership, even though CSOs and government officials in the Burkinabe health sector have bought into the dominant philosophy of development and thus feel that donors are necessary. Conceding that the county is poor, with few resources, there is no more imagining an alternative that aligns with what the country has to offer, but rather an unyielding view of Burkina Faso and Burkinabe as lagging in development and struggling to catch up.

Although Burkina Faso implemented very similar neoliberal development policies as Kenya after Sankara's death in 1987, revolutionary ideas of development and self-reliance continue to tacitly inform the Burkinabe rendering of ownership. Burkinabe stakeholders conceptualize *ownership* as the individual acting with the greater community's interest in mind. Alternatively, the Kenyan and donor definitions of ownership are embedded in the technical language of neoliberal development, where the state takes responsibility for development policies and consults civil society and donors throughout the development process. These two disparate conceptualizations of ownership remain rooted in each country's particular political history, illustrating how in a supposedly apolitical and universal paradigm, politics continue to permeate development. In contrast, Sankara's lasting legacy in Burkina Faso insinuates a potential to rupture the current development paradigm and replace it with a more just and equitable alternative.

Conclusion

Claims regarding a change in development practices based on a new model of ownership in Africa are untenable. The principles of ownership, donor-partnership, evidence-driven development, and long-term development strategies are just some of the indicators of the reigning set of assumptions about political, economic, and social progress underpinning the ownership paradigm. Burkina Faso and Kenya have both adopted these assumptions and the corresponding discourses and practices into their domestic frameworks for development. Consequently, both countries manifest similar outcomes: Donors as a community of development experts who, despite their considerable authority over development-policy options, remain impervious to criticism and unaccountable for failed policies. Under the ownership paradigm, Kenya and Burkina Faso also remain underdeveloped subjects. I have shown that Burkinabe community-level family planning policies and techniques come directly from the donors and the government, which constructs the men and women who do not employ donor-legitimized family planning methods as traditional and blames them for stalling development. I have demonstrated how underdevelopment manifests at the state level in Kenya, where despite exhibiting commitment to the discourses and practices of the ownership paradigm, donors continue to regard the Kenyan government as untrustworthy and lacking ownership. Thus, the nature of the Kenyan government-donor relationship is more characteristic of paternalism than partnership.

Politics are still relevant in Burkina Faso and Kenya. Stakeholders' statements about what ownership means highlighted not only the different ways in which they conceptualized ownership, but also how those conceptualizations are informed by the particular political histories of each country, more specifically the political climates that characterized each country during the initial moment of structural adjustments in Africa. Irrespective of their different understandings of ownership, the dominant language still permeates and influences state and civil society engagement with development in a way that is consistent across both Burkina Faso and Kenya. However, the lingering ideas informing the Burkinabe version of ownership suggest the potential for escaping the ownership paradigm in Africa and, as Frantz Fanon stated, setting afoot a new humanity (Fanon 1961).

Notes

1 *Bailleurs de fond* is another word for donor.
2 BS3007, 30/07/2015_Ouagadougou.
3 0056 CSO, 15/01/2016_Nairboi.
4 I give examples of this in both the Burkina and Kenya chapters, highlighting in the governments' policy documents how they outline the cost of implementing their health strategies and consistently fall short of meeting these identified amounts, requiring more donor financial inputs. Furthermore, the problem of funding is evident in the calls by the World Health Organization and UN, along with other donors, for more financial commitments to health from governments in order to meet MDGs and SDGs.
5 This is from a conversation that I had working in the World Bank office around 5pm on July 8, 2015 in Ouagadougou. The conversation happened in French. In

order to capture everything that the IT specialist was saying, I paraphrased the longer conversation in English from the original French.
6 0050Donor, 05/01/2016_Nairobi.
7 BS3007, 30/07/2015_Ouagadougou.
8 0056CSO, 00/01/2016_Nairobi.
9 YB0729, 07/29/2015_Tenkodogo.
10 0051Donor, 00/01/2016_Nairobi.
11 Ibid.
12 DR0107, 01/07/2015_Ouagadougou.
13 Ibid.
14 0049MoH, 04/01/2016_Nairobi.
15 LB0709, 09/07/2015_Ouagadougou.
16 This participant observation is based on a conversation that I had on July 7, 2015, around 8:30 p.m. in Koudougou, Burkina Faso.
17 This participant observation comes from a conversation that took place on July 24, 2015, around noon in Tenkodogo, Burkina Faso.

References

Alemazung, Joy Asongazoh. 2010. "Post-Colonial Colonialism: An Analysis of International Factors and Actors Marring African Socio-Economic and Political Development." *The Journal of Pan African Studies* 3 (10): 62–84.

Brown, Stephen. 2001. "Authoritarian Leaders and Multiparty Elections in Africa: How Foreign Donors Help to Keep Kenya's Daniel Arap Moi in Power." *Third World Quarterly* 22 (5): 725–39.

Buiter, Willem. 2007. "Country Ownership, A Term Whose Time Has Gone." *Development in Practice* 17 (4–5): 647–52.

Cooper, Frederick. 1997. "Modernizing Bureaucrats, Backward Africans, and the Development Concepts." In *International Development and the Social Sciences: Essays on the History and Politics of Knowledge*, edited by Frederick Cooper and Randall M. Packard, 64–92. Berkeley: University of California Press.

de Renzio, Paolo, Lindsay Whitfield, and Isaline Bergamaschi. 2008. "Reforming Foreign Aid Practices: What Country Ownership is and What Donors Can Do to Support It." www.researchgate.net/publication/30527504_Reforming_Foreign_Aid_Practices_What_country_ownership_is_and_what_donors_can_do_to_support_it.

Devarajan, Shantayanan, David R. Dollar, and Torgny Holmgren. 2001. *Aid and Reform in Africa: Lessons from Ten Case Studies*. Washington, DC: World Bank Publications.

Esteva, Gustavo. 1996. "Development." In *The Development Dictionary: A Guide to Knowledge as Power*, edited by Wolfgang Sachs, 6–25. London: Zed.

Fanon, Frantz. 1961. *The Wretched of the Earth*. Grove/Atlantic, Inc. New York.

Ferguson, James. 2006. *Global Shadows: Africa in the Neoliberal World Order*. Durham, NC: Duke University Press.

Gabas, Jean-Jaques, Y. A. Faure, and A. Sindzingre. 1997. "The Effectiveness of French Aid-Burkina Faso." In *Foreign Aid in Africa: Learning from Country*

Experience, edited by Nicolas van de Walle, Jerker Carlsson, and Gloria Somolekae, 36–64. Uppsala: Nordic Africa Institute.

Grovogui, Siba N. 2001. "Come to Africa: A Hermeneutics of Race in International Theory." *Alternatives: Global, Local, Political* 26 (4): 425–48.

Haas, Peter M. 1989. "Do Regimes Matter? Epistemic Communities and Mediterranean Pollution Control." *International Organization* 43 (3): 377–403.

Hanmer, Lucia, Ikiara Gerrishon, Walter Eberlei, and Carolyn Abong. 2003. "Kenya." In *Fighting Poverty in Africa: Are PRSPs Making a Difference*, edited by David Booth, 91–119. London: Overseas Development Institute.

Harper-Shipman, T.D. 2018. "La Santé Avant Tout (Health before Everything)." In *A Certain Amount of Madness: The Life Politics and Legacies of Thomas Sankara*, edited by Amber Murrey, 1st ed. Pluto Press. London.

Harsch, Ernest. 2013. "The Legacies of Thomas Sankara: A Revolutionary Experience in Retrospect." *Review of African Political Economy* 40 (137): 358–74.

———. 2014. *Thomas Sankara: An African Revolutionary*. Athens, OH: Ohio University Press.

Keita, L. D., ed. 2011. *Philosophy and African Development: Theory and Practice*. Dakar, Senegal: Codesria.

Maathai, Wangari. 2008. *Unbowed: A Memoir*. New York: Random House Digital, Inc.

Martin, Guy. 1987. "Ideology and Praxis in Thomas Sankara's Populist Revolution of 4 August 1983 in Burkina Faso." *Issue: A Journal of Opinion* 15: 77–90.

Ministère de l'Economie et des Finances. 2011. "Burkina Faso SCADD: Stratégie de Croissance Accélérée et de Développment Durable 2011–2015." www.unpei. org/sites/default/files/e_library_documents/Burkina_Faso_PRSP_2011.pdf.

Ministry of Health. 2012. "Kenya National Health Accounts 2012/13." www.health policyproject.com/pubs/523_KenyaNHA.pdf.

Ministry of State for Planning, National Development and Vision 2030. 2008. "First Medium Term Plan (2008–2012): Kenya Vision 2030: A Globally Competitive and Prosperous Kenya." http://vision2030.go.ke/inc/uploads/2018/06/kenya_medium_term_plan_2008-2012-1.pdf.

Mkandawire, Thandika. 2014. "The Spread of Economic Doctrines and Policymaking in Postcolonial Africa." *African Studies Review* 57 (1): 171–98.

Moi, Daniel Arap. 1986. *Kenya African Nationalism: Nyayo Philosophy and Principles*. London: Macmillan.

Muga, Richard, Paul Kizito, Michael Mbayah, and Terry Gakuruh. 2005. "Overview of the Health System in Kenya." *Kenya Service Provision Assessment Survey 2004*, 13–26. Nairobi, Kenya: National Coordinating Agency for Population and Development, Ministry of Health, Central Bureau of Statistics, and ORC Macro.

National Treasury. 2014. "Development Estimates 2014/15." Republic of Kenya, National Treasury. http://e-promis.treasury.go.ke/portal/wp-content/uploads/2015/06/ERD-Hand-Book-2014_2015.pdf.

Obadina, Tunde. 2014. *Population and Overcrowding*. Broomall, PA: National Highlights, Inc.

OECD. 2008. "Third High Level Forum on Aid Effectiveness: Accra Agenda for Action." www.oecd.org/dac/effectiveness/theaccrahighlevelforumhlf3andtheac craagendaforaction.htm.

OECD. 2011. *Aid Effectiveness 2005–10: Progress in Implementing the Paris Declaration.* OECD Publishing.

Okereke, Chukwumerije, and Patricia Agupusi. 2015. *Homegrown Development in Africa: Reality or Illusion?* Abingdon: Routledge.

Owusu, Francis. 2006. "Discourse on Development from Dependency to Neoliberalism." In *Beyond the "African Tragedy": Discourses on Development and the Global Economy,* edited by Malinda Smith, 25–48. Hampshire: Ashgate Publishing.

Paris Declaration. 2012. "Accra Agenda for Action." Paris, OECD. www.oecd.org/dac/effectiveness/34428351.pdf.

Pender, John. 2001. "From Structural Adjustment to Comprehensive Development Framework: Conditionality Transformed?" *Third World Quarterly* 22 (3): 397–411.

Pierson, Paul. 1993. "When Effect Becomes Cause: Policy Feedback and Political Change." *World Politics* 45 (4): 595–628.

Ravindran, Sundari T. K. 2014. "Poverty, Food Security and Universal Access to Sexual and Reproductive Health Services: A Call for Cross-Movement Advocacy against Neoliberal Globalisation." *Reproductive Health Matters* 22 (43): 14–27.

Rono, Joseph Kipkemboi. 2002. "The Impact of Structural Adjustment Programmes on Kenyan Society." *Journal of Social Development in Africa* 17 (1): 81.

Sankara, Thomas. 1985. "The 'Political Orientation' of Burkina Faso." *Review of African Political Economy* 12 (32): 48–55.

Savadogo, Kimseyinga and Claude Wetta. 1991. "The Impact of Self-imposed Adjustment: The Case of Burkina Faso, 1983–1989." ww.unicef-irc.org/publications/141-the-impact-of-self-imposed-adjustment-the-case-of-burkina-faso-1983–1989.html.

Smith, David. 2015. "Burkina Faso's Revolutionary Hero Thomas Sankara to Be Exhumed." *The Guardian,* March 6, 2015, sec. World news. www.theguardian.com/world/2015/mar/06/burkina-fasos-revolutionary-hero-thomas-sankara-to-be-exhumed.

Smith, James Howard. 2008. *Bewitching Development: Witchcraft and the Reinvention of Development in Neoliberal Kenya.* Chicago: University of Chicago Press.

Thelen, Kathleen. 1999. "Historical Institutionalism in Comparative Politics." *Annual Review of Political Science* 2 (1): 369–404.

United States Government. 2014. *Kenya: Country Development Cooperation Strategy: 2014–18: Sustainably Transforming Kenya's Governance and Economy.* Washington, DC: United States Agency for International Development.

Weeks, John, David Andersson, Chris Cramer, Geda Alemayehu, Hailu Degol, Frank Muhereza, Matteo Rizzi, Eric Ronge, and Howard Stein. 2002. "Supporting Ownership: Swedish Development Cooperation with Kenya, Tanzania, and Uganda." Sida Evaluation 02/33:1. www.oecd.org/countries/tanzania/35203817.pdf.

Whitfield, Lindsay, ed. 2009. *The Politics of Aid: African Strategies for Dealing with Donors*. New York: Oxford University Press.

Wilkins, Michael. 1989. "The Death of Thomas Sankara and the Rectification of the People's Revolution in Burkina Faso." *African Affairs* 88 (352): 375–88.

Wolfensohn, James D. 2005. *Voice for the World's Poor: Selected Speeches and Writings of World Bank President James D. Wolfensohn, 1995–2005*. Vol. 889. Washington, DC: World Bank Publications.

Wolfensohn, James D. 1998. "The Other Crisis". Address to the Board of Governors, World Bank/IMF Annual Meetings, Washington, DC: World Bank Publications.

Wolfensohn, James D., and Stanley Fischer. 2000. "The Comprehensive Development Framework (CDF) and Poverty Reduction Strategy Papers (PRSP): Joint Note by James D. Wolfensohn and Stanley Fischer." www.imf.org/external/np/prsp/pdf/cdfprsp.pdf.

World Bank. 2003. *Toward Country-Led Development: A Multi-Partner Evaluation of the Comprehensive Development Framework*. Washington, DC: World Bank Group.

Zagré, Pascal. 1994. *Les Politiques Économiques du Burkina Faso: Une tradition d'ajustement structurel*. Paris: KARTHALA Editions.

Conclusion
Go back and get it

Let us not look back at what has happened in the past; let us look forward.
 – James Wolfensohn, to African leaders in Addis Ababa

Se wo were fi na wosankofa a yenkyi. (It is not wrong to go back for that which you have forgotten.)
 – Sankofa Proverb

"Donors want governments in the driver's seat, but they want to hold on to the road map." These words, plastered on the wall in the Kenyan official's office, like those of former World Bank President Wolfensohn (2005), evoke the future-oriented language and practices embedded in the ownership paradigm and reveal the power relations that determine who is the implementer and the knower of development on the road towards ownership. Drivers merely follow the rules and already established, sanctioned roads. The average driver had no say in where to pave a new road or put up a new stop sign. Perhaps that the driver is only a chauffeur, taking direction from an employer. In the end, being in the driver's seat does not automatically translate into countries having power over their development possibilities, as the approved roads have already been paved. More important than being behind the wheel or even holding the map is designing the map. The map indicates the legitimate courses and avenues one can take to reach a destination.

A cursory reading of the previous chapters leaves one with little hope in the ownership paradigm's potential to deliver genuinely African solutions to Africa's development problems. The paradigm is, however, useful in constructing African problems that will require Western solutions. Despite formal measures and language of ownership suggesting a relativistic approach to development, in Kenya and Burkina Faso subscribing to the ownership paradigm results in similar outcomes. In both countries the language and application of the OECD's version of ownership designates donors as knowledge experts, indispensable to national development processes, but it does not have an internal mechanism for holding donors accountable. What, then, are the consequences of Africa *owning* development? Is there an alternative? And how does the aid-dependent African state make steps towards this end?

Ownership is not context-specific; it represents another universal development model. There is a cocktail of global development initiatives from Millennium Development Goals to Sustainable Development Goals, and other international development markers embedded in the paradigm. Because African governments are implored to adopt these as development ends or forgo funding, it is difficult to see how development is truly contextual.[1] More importantly, the means and the ends of policy are not country-specific. Burkina Faso and Kenya use PRSPs, SWAps, MTFEs, and other donor-sanctioned frameworks for social and economic progress, which is measured in terms of poverty reduction in both countries. Donors working in both countries have assumed the formal role of knowledge experts and are formally institutionalized as development partners in rhetoric and practices like donor-working groups and aid-effectiveness secretariats, stakeholders who actively work to change state and civil society. Using supposedly consensual knowledge embedded in PRSPs and other donor-driven development tools, they work to build country capacity. The power derived from donor's consensual knowledge is evident in the prominence of evidence-based and measurable strategies in development policies. That neither country meets donors' development targets serves to maintain the epistemic community of donors and perpetuate the notion of a perpetual development crisis. Ever-impending economic, environmental, or social crises validate the need for donor expertise in both countries.

Although donors have considerable influence in the domestic affairs of Kenya and Burkina Faso, their position as knowledge experts absolves them of any responsibility for past or future development failures in either, while guaranteeing them an indispensable role in the domestic affairs of both. When I asked civil society, government, and donor representatives who is held responsible when policies do not achieve their stated objectives, nearly every respondent named the government, revealing how adoption of the ownership principles assigns responsibility for development. Even if the formal language of the Paris Declaration suggests that there be mutual accountability across stakeholders, on the ground this is not the case because donors are cast as merely contributing expertise and capacity support. In this light, it is difficult for national stakeholders to hold donors accountable for what seems like the government's failed development policies and initiatives.

In turn, the current development paradigm fosters a sense of underdevelopment in both countries, but this was especially salient in Burkina Faso. Burkinabe development stakeholders view themselves as underdeveloped, requiring financial and epistemic aid from donors to achieve development. Underdevelopment is not just a matter of absent local resources and expertise; it is a reinforced mindset. Family planning policies and implementation show how the ownership paradigm facilitates the reproduction of the underdeveloped subject in Burkina Faso and further points to internal factors (such as a woman's choice to have more than three children) as stifling development. Similarly, in Kenya donors refuse to recognize the government as a veritable development partner even though it demonstrates a full command of the development lexis, from the underlying economic doctrines to the use of ownership discourses. If it were the case that the government was an actual partner, the Kenyan government should have the autonomy to reject implementation of agreed-upon policies if they turn out to be inappropriate. Instead, donors view the Government of Kenya's (GoK) default as a lack of commitment to development, an indication that donors must continue to monitor it.

Where there is variation under the ownership paradigm is at the level of semantics. Stakeholders in both countries define ownership according to their respective histories and critical moments in development. While Burkinabe stakeholders voiced a relatively cohesive view of ownership (i.e. each individual understanding their responsibility within, and to, the community in the name of collective progress), Kenyan stakeholders understood ownership relative to their defined roles under the conventional development paradigm. The Kenyan government viewed ownership as government being in the driver's seat but accepting help from donors. Kenyan civil society representatives defined ownership as being involved in every stage of the policy process, from formulation to implementation. Each version of ownership harkens back to the countries' development commitments at the time that the World Bank and IMF were introducing SAPs in Africa. The permeation of these ideas and the politics they represent suggest that politics still matter. As the current development paradigm seeks to make notions of progress seem apolitical and objective, these conflicting interpretations suggest that the paradigm has not yet reached hegemonic status.

What is there to own?

As I demonstrate throughout this book, the problems with ownership are rooted in the promises of development *ipso facto*. The ownership paradigm does not pretend to rupture the scientific coloniality that has long been the adhesive binding colonialism and development in Africa (Mignolo 2009,

2002; Gyekye and Wiredu 1992). The shift of accountability from donors to national stakeholders is especially pernicious with respect to reproductive policies, in that the burden of "development" and of addressing the unequal distribution of resources needed to improve women's capacities falls principally on Burkinabe women themselves instead of states or private sector actors.

The ownership paradigm raises the stakes of development in Kenya and Burkina Faso. With the governments and societies accepting full responsibility for the range of development policies that they are implementing, if these countries continue to see limited progress fifty years from now, there may be further justification for the types of neotrusteeships that some scholars have proposed for Africa.[2] And some see that critical moment arriving sooner. In a recent study, Ian Taylor (2016) argues that Africa is headed for another economic crisis because the continent remains trapped in a "resource corner" that precludes industrialization across the continent. Those who praise the continent's recent economic growth laud the amelioration in policies, institutions, and governance as responsible for the continent's success. Taylor, however, counters and demonstrates that it is increased natural resource extraction across the continent that accounts for the ostensible increase in GDP. He further argues that the boom in natural resource prices due to the emerging economies' growing industrialization has aided Africa's economic growth. With the continued reliance on raw material exports and imported finished products, the continent will not be able to industrialize and thus will remain in the same structurally disadvantaged place as when Africa was the "hopeless continent."

The constant association of Africa with crisis, real or imagined, further perpetuates the racist discourse underlying the call for good governance and overdue interventions in the domestic and regional affairs on the continent (Anievas, Manchanda, and Shilliam 2015). Siba Grovogui aptly decodes the West's inscription in pop culture and scholarship as possessing "cultural adaptability, political competency, and ethical versatility," while Africa represents an "internal dysfunction" that impedes political, social, and, most importantly, economic development because its static cultural institutions are not conducive to "good governance" (2001, 427). The development impasse in Africa thus becomes primordial. Even if African governments *own* development, they will continue to lag behind the West and be held responsible for their own "underdevelopment."

An accurate reading of contemporary Africa is incomplete without accounting for the remnants of the colonial system embedded in the development industry. By incorporating the history of colonialism and its lingering power structures within donor relations in Africa, the notion of "ownership" as emancipatory and paradigm-shifting seems almost a cruel joke. By contrast, "ownership" as another scheme that brands Africa as underdeveloped, in crisis, and perpetually in need of donor assistance is more apt. As such, several research questions remain for future scholars and practitioners interested in understanding the implications of ownership in Africa. For example, how does the initial moment of structural adjustments influence conceptualizations of ownership in other African countries? Researchers might also delve deeper into African civil societies and their negotiations of ownership vis-à-vis the state and donors.

Moving beyond ownership

When former World Bank President James Wolfensohn addressed a room filled with African leaders in Addis Ababa in 1998, imploring them not to look back but only to the future, he captured the underlying spirit of ownership. My analysis of the language and practice of ownership in Burkina Faso and Kenya reveals active attempts to ahistoricize the centuries of exploitation and extortion that the continent has endured (Rodney 1974; Keita 2011). To truly consent to development at this juncture is not merely to look back but also to follow the Sankofa proverb and "go back and get it," "it" being a more profound sense of social and political change that coalesces around each country's realities. "It" refers to the demand that African leaders and societies once placed on the West to acknowledge its role in under-developing and exploiting the continent.[3] The possibility of "going back" problematizes the continuities across donor-driven development paradigms. In Burkina Faso "going back" may also demonstrate how development and its associated family planning methods remain rooted in the racist and misogynistic logic of Malthusian political economy. African governments "going back" could prevent donors and the international community from acting as the sole arbiters of history.

Currently, the ownership paradigm, with its call for government accountability and commitment to development strategies and goals based on donor priorities, does not permit Africans to go back. Bringing the history of exploitation to bear on the ownership paradigm undermines it, as the paradigm cannot reconcile the reality "going back" exposes. True reconciliation with the past would require donors to acknowledge the ways in which predatory African states are a legacy of colonialism (Young 1994; Mamdani 1996; Lange 2004; Migdal 1988). It means tackling the reality of the African state, as Makau Mutua argues:

> At its dawn, the African postcolonial state was handed a virtually impossible task: Assimilate the norms of the liberal tradition overnight

within the structures of the colonial state while at the same time building a nation from disparate groups in a hostile international political economy.

(2008, 28)

Understanding the African state through this historical lens forecloses attempts to characterize the political corruption and weak states in Africa as reflective of an inescapable, innate disposition. This rendering of the African state would also force former colonizers, who are now donors, to struggle with the beast that they created – not as saviors but in humble atonement. "Going back" is the first step toward decolonizing ownership.

Decolonizing ownership entails opening a space for different versions of heath and development and a wide range of experts and tools. I do not mean to suggest that things like health, education, and decent housing should no longer be important goals of African societies. However, what constitutes being healthy, having a good education, and living in decent housing should not be the product of another culture's notions.

When African governments and societies engage in the process of defining their political, economic, and social trajectories, there is no need for external actors to measure the level of country ownership. When African countries have embarked on this journey, however, the West has intervened because the outcomes of genuine ownership can conflict with Western interests. Thomas Sankara's thwarted revolution is but one of many examples.[4] Under Sankara's leadership, Burkinabe worked towards achieving a standard of progress based on the cultural, economic, and political resources available in Burkina Faso. The Sankara administration encouraged them to consume locally produced foods in lieu of imported European products. Civil servants had to wear locally made traditional garb to work instead of suits and ties (Harsch 2014; Sankara 1985). Requiring Burkinabe to consume what they produced was not solely a matter of economic doctrine; it was a step towards mental decolonization. In an interview regarding his administration's progress after his first year in office, Sankara acknowledged the persistent neocolonial spirit in Burkina Faso: "The most important thing for us, however, is not what is lacking. Most important is the effort we have made to change people's attitudes" (Sankara 2007, n.p.). As Sankara and the Burkinabe were defining progress through the prism of their historical realities, uneasy Western powers supported his opponent Blaise Campaoré, whose troops assassinated the revolutionary leader (Harsch 2014). The Burkinabe revolution nonetheless highlights the potential as well as the pitfalls of opposing a dominant development paradigm.

The epistemic and financial dependency embedded in ownership is not new. As Paulin Hountondji observes,

> it was natural that the annexation of the Third World, its integration in the worldwide capitalist system through trade and colonization, also comprises a "scientific" window, that the draining of material riches goes hand in hand with intellectual and scientific exploitation.
>
> (1992, 242)

There is indeed a scientific exploitation evident in the ownership paradigm and neoliberal development. Donors propagate the ownership paradigm and its associated tools and measures as objective and scientifically guaranteed to produce results if implemented properly. However, tools like SWAps, PRSPs, and even the measures of poverty emanating from the World Bank have been criticized for having little empirical basis (Owa 2015; Wade 2004; Hill 2002; Lazarus 2008). Thus, contesting the notion of ownership that arises from the consensual knowledge of an epistemic community of donors is a crucial starting point for breaking down and delegitimizing the paradigm itself (Mignolo 2002). African thinkers have posited what this process looks like in practice.[5]

Moving beyond ownership means moving beyond the language, practice, and promises of neocolonialist development in Africa. Addressing the social needs specific to each African country cannot happen under a universal approach that gives *ex ante* prescriptions for progress. A decolonized ownership may mean uncertainty, but it offers more opportunities for transformation. More equitable, just, and humane solutions may mean the dissolution of the state or a strengthening of state capacity. Economic progress may require the abolition of private property rights or stronger mechanisms for their enforcement. Women's empowerment may mean allowing a woman to have more than three children and ensuring that she is not shamed for doing so. Decolonizing ownership opens possibilities.

Notes

1 Despite the difference in contexts, both Kenya and Burkina Faso implement the same type of aggressive population control policies, although the demographics and demand for family planning differ significantly between them. In Burkina Faso, not only is there limited adoption of family planning, but the low prevalence coalesces around the limited desire for family planning across the Burkinabe population. In contrast, Kenya has a longer history of engagement with family planning policies and has seen dramatic increases in the indicators around population control.

2 In the 1990s with the "so-called" collapse of various African states, a small community of scholars advocated for the formal recolonization of Africa in the interest of protecting Africans (see Mazrui 1994; Pfaff 1995). The increased control of African states by external forces eventually took on more palatable names like, proxy governance, neotrusteeship, and shared-sovereignty (see Lemay-Hébert 2015).

3 For example, the Lagos Plan of Action is a development strategy that African leaders drafted and adopted in the 1980s which identified Cold War politics, colonialism, and the global economic architecture as responsible for impeding Africa's development (Organization of African Unity 1985).

4 Another notable example of African ownership being truncated occurred during the prime ministership of Patrice Lumumba, in 1960, in the Republic of the Congo, as it was then called. Belgium and the U.S. did not approve of Lumumba's seemingly socialist policies and his unwillingness to grant independence to the Katanga region. Shortly after Lumumba took office, Belgium and the U.S. colluded to overthrow him. He was shortly thereafter assassinated, and Mobutu Sese Seko assumed power and went on to serve Western interests during his thirty years in power and, simultaneously, to exploit the Congolese people (Witte 2001; Gerard and Kuklick 2015).

5 Among the African writers and activists who have called for Africans to "know thyself" are Ngũgĩ wa Thiong'o (1994), who illustrates how language and literature in Africa must be de-linked from European values. Similarly, Wangari Maathai explores the need to escape the cultural nihilism that comes with defining educational success in Africa in terms of how well one excels in European language and history (Maathai 1995).

References

Anievas, Alexander, Nivi Manchanda, and Robbie Shilliam, eds. 2015. *Race and Racism in International Relations: Confronting the Global Colour Line*. Oxfordshire, England: Routledge.

Gerard, Emmanuel, and Bruce Kuklick. 2015. *Death in the Congo: Murdering Patrice Lumumba*. Cambridge, MA: Harvard University Press.

Grovogui, Siba N. 2001. "Come to Africa: A Hermeneutics of Race in International Theory." *Alternatives: Global, Local, Political* 26 (4): 425–48.

Gyekye, Kwame, and Kwasi Wiredu. 1992. *Person and Community Ghanaian Philosophical Studies I*. Cultural Heritage and Contemporary Change Series. Washington, DC: Council for Research in Values.

Harsch, Ernest. 2014. *Thomas Sankara: An African Revolutionary*. Athens: Ohio University Press.

Hill, Peter S. 2002. "The Rhetoric of Sector-Wide Approaches for Health Development." *Social Science & Medicine* 54 (11): 1725–37.

Hountondji, Paulin. 1992. "Recapture." In *The Surreptitious Speech: Presence Africaine and the Politics of Otherness 1947–1987*, edited by V. Y. Mudimbe. Chicago: University of Chicago Press.

Keita, L. D., ed. 2011. *Philosophy and African Development: Theory and Practice*. Dakar, Senegal: Codesria.

Lange, Matthew K. 2004. "British Colonial Legacies and Political Development." *World Development* 32 (6): 905–22.

Lazarus, Joel. 2008. "Participation in Poverty Reduction Strategy Papers: Reviewing the Past, Assessing the Present and Predicting the Future." *Third World Quarterly* 29 (6): 1205–21.

Lemay-Hébert, Nicolas. 2015. "State Building, Neocolonialism and Neotrusteeships." In *Handbook of International Security and Development*, edited by Paul Jackson, 95–111. Cheltenham: Edward Elgar.

Maathai, Wangari. 1995. "Bottlenecks to Development in Africa." Greenbeltmovement.Com. August 30, 1995. /wangari-maathai/key-speeches-and-articles/bottleknecks-to-development-in-africa.

Mamdani, Mahmood. 1996. *Citizen and Subject: Contemporary African and the Legacy of Late Colonialism*. Princeton: Princeton University Press.

Mazrui, Ali. 1994. "Development or Recolonization?" *New Perspectives Quarterly* 11 (4): 18–19.

Migdal, Joel S. 1988. *Strong Societies and Weak States: State-Society Relations and State Capabilities in the Third World*. Princeton: Princeton University Press.

Mignolo, Walter. 2002. "The Geopolitics of Knowledge and the Colonial Difference." *The South Atlantic Quarterly* 101 (1): 57–96.

———. 2009. "Epistemic Disobedience, Independent Thought and Decolonial Freedom." *Theory, Culture & Society* 26 (7–8): 159–81.

Mutua, Makau. 2008. "Human Rights in Africa: The Limited Promise of Liberalism." *African Studies Review* 51 (1): 17–39.

Organization of African Unity. 1985. "Lagos Plan of Action for Economic Development of Africa: 1980–2000." Addis Ababa: Organization of African Unity.

Owa, Masumi. 2015. "Is OECD DAC's Aid Effectiveness Agenda Based on Evidence?" *Journal of Development Effectiveness* 7 (4): 435–44.

Pfaff, William. 1995. "A New Colonialism? Europe Must Go Back into Africa." *Foreign Affairs* 74 (1): 2–6.

Rodney, Walter. 1974. *How Europe Underdeveloped Africa*. Washington, DC: Howard University Press.

Sankara, Thomas. 1985. "The 'Political Orientation' of Burkina Faso." *Review of African Political Economy* 12 (32): 48–55.

———. 2007. *Thomas Sankara Speaks: The Burkina Faso Revolution 1983–1987*. 2nd ed. New York: Pathfinder Press.

Taylor, Ian. 2016. "Dependency Redux: Why Africa Is Not Rising." *Review of African Political Economy* 43 (147): 8–25.

Thiong'o, Ngũgĩ wa. 1994. *Decolonising the Mind: The Politics of Language in African Literature*. Nairobi, Kenya: East African Publishers.

Wade, Robert Hunter. 2004. "Is Globalization Reducing Poverty and Inequality?" *World Development* 32 (4): 567–89.

Witte, Ludo de. 2001. *The Assassination of Lumumba*. London: Verso.

Wolfensohn, James D. 2005. *Voice for the World's Poor: Selected Speeches and Writings of World Bank President James D. Wolfensohn, 1995–2005*. Vol. 889. Washington, DC: World Bank Publications.

Young, Crawford. 1994. *The African Colonial State in Comparative Perspective*. New Haven: Yale University Press.

Index

Abuja Declaration 43, 67
accountability 120–1; for ownership 80–1, 118–19
Accra Agenda for Action (AAA) 21, 93–4, 97, 105
actors 8; civil society organizations (CSOs) 9–10; *see also* local actors
adjustment loans 5
Africa: Abuja Declaration 43, 67; association with crisis 119; Bamako Initiative (BI) 42–43; capacity building in 21; colonialism 118–20; economics, influence on development 96; governance in 9; health sector 30–1; history of exploitation 120–1; local actors 19; moving beyond ownership 122; overpopulation 60–1; as owner of development 117; underdevelopment in 103–6, 118–19
African Socialism 109
aid *see* donors; foreign aid
alignment 6, 85

Bamako Initiative (BI) 42, 43
bilateral donors 56, 74, 83, 97, 100
Booth, David, on ownership 26
Bretton Woods 5
budget support 21
Burkina Faso 2–4, 8, 12, 20–21, 28, 30, 33, 35n6, 92; adoption of the ownership paradigm 44; Bamako Initiative (BI) 43; *Cadre stratégique de lutte contre la pauvreté* ('Strategic Framework for Poverty Reduction'

(CLSP)) 43–4; civil society 94; civil society actors 10; civil society organizations (CSOs) 47–50; community self-help projects 109; community-based organizations (CBOs) 31, 53–4; consolidation of the language of ownership 94; *Direction générale de l'économie et de la planification* (DGEP) 46; donor influence 54–7; donors 93–4; donors' definition of ownership 45–6; drug prices 42; family planning 57–61, 61–2; fieldwork in 28–9; five-year development plans 43; global health initiatives 100; government definition of ownership 46–7; health policy 100; health sector 97; health sector development indicators 51–2; heath system 48; international donors 42; *La lettre d'intention de politique de développement humain durable* ('Letter of Intent on Sustainable Human Development Policy' (LIPDHD)) 43; *La stratégie de croissance accélérée et de développement durable* ('The Strategy for Accelerated Growth and Sustainable Development' (SCADD)) 44, 52, 57; *l'appropriation de developpement* 106; *l'appropriation nationale* 44; *Le Cadre stratégique de lutte contre la pauvreté* 43; local actors 93; Millennium Development

Goals (MDGs) 100; movements 47–8; *National Family Planning Stimulus Plan 2013–2015* 58, 60; non-governmental organizations (NGOs) 29; ownership in 19, 41, 50, 110, 120; partnerships 94, 100; policy-makers 100; politics in 111; population control policies 122n1; Poverty Reduction Strategy Papers (PRSPs) 50–1, 99; *Programme d'Appui au Développement Sanitaire* (PADS) 48, 52–4; *Programme Populaire de Développement* ('People's Development Program' (PPD)) 43; *Renforcement de Capacités* (RENCAP) 52–3; responsibility for policy outcomes 102–3; Sankara regime 107–8, 121; scientific capitalism 18; structural adjustment programs (SAPs) 106, 108; supranational organizations 42; top-down development 45; underdevelopment in 50–2, 103–6, 118; Vision 2020 93
Busan Partnership for Effective Development Cooperation 6
Bush administration 5

Cadre stratégique de lutte contre la pauvreté ('Strategic Framework for Poverty Reduction' (CLSP)) 43–4
Campaoré, Blaise 121
capacity building 20, 21, 98
Carlsson, J. 26–7
case selection 29–31; geography 35n6
challengers 10–11
civil society 10–11, 27–8, 30, 34, 87; interviews from 41; involvement in ownership of Kenya's development 74–6; ownership in 18
civil society organizations (CSOs) 9–10, 21, 28, 31, 84, 95; in Burkina Faso 47–50; definition of ownership 75; in Kenya 72; monitoring function of 74
Clark, Helen 16–17, 19
Clinton, Hillary 17; on ownership 16
coloniality 17
community self-help projects 109

community-based organizations (CBOs) 3–4, 10, 29, 52–4; in Burkina Faso 31
Compaoré, Blaise 50, 108
Comprehensive Development Framework (CDF) 5–7, 98–9
consensual knowledge 22, 117
consolidation of the language of ownership 93–5
contraceptives *see* family planning
Cooper, Fredrick 104
country ownership 1, 2, 26
crisis of global poverty 99
critical discourse analysis 29

Danish International Development Agency (DANIDA) 29, 68
data collection: from sources in Burkina Faso 41, 46–50; from sources in Kenya 68–9
decolonial theory 11, 17, 18, 20
decolonizing ownership 121, 122
definition of ownership 45; in Burkinabe civil society 48–50; donors' 45–6; government 46–7; *see also* ownership
dependency embedded in ownership 122
development 1, 2, 4, 11, 12, 18; Africa as owner of 117; in Burkina Faso 42; civil society organizations (CSOs) 9–10; Comprehensive Development Framework (CDF) 5; discourse in 20–1; discourses 8; donor influence over 56–7; funding 95; "going back" 120–1; homegrown 8–9; influence of economics on 96; International Conference on Financing for Development 5; Lagos Plan of Action 123n3; long-term strategies 7, 44, 93, 101, 105; market approach to 105, 109; Medium-Term Expenditure Frameworks (MTEFs) 7–8; neoliberal 42, 50, 72, 103, 106, 107–10, 109, 122; *nyayo* 107, 109; OECD definition of ownership 2; ownership 3, 16–17, 68–9; partnerships 79–86; political economy analysis (PEA) 31–3; Sankara's model of 107–8, 110;

self-reliant 20, 108–9; stakeholder participation in Kenya 71–2; stakeholders 9; state-led 4; top-down 45; U.S. Agency for International Development (USAID) 5
development partners 94
Development Partnership Forum Meetings (DPFs) 83
discourse 6, 8, 20–1, 29, 33; in development 20–1; in economics 96; in ownership 19
donors 2, 4, 7, 10–12, 12n2, 16, 20, 25, 26, 27–8, 81, 84, 92, 96, 116, 117, 122; alignment 85; bilateral 56, 74, 83, 97, 100; and coloniality 17; definition of ownership 45–6; and epistemic communities 23; as epistemic community 76–8; as experts 10, 11, 76, 96, 97, 98, 111; and family planning 57–61; financial impact on health sectors 101–2; harmonization 6, 85; influence of 54–7; institutionalization 78; interviews 29, 41; Japanese International Cooperation Agency (JICA) 97; to Kenya's development 73–4; longevity 78–80; Medium-Term Expenditure Frameworks (MTEFs) 7–8; multilateral 34–5n5, 56, 100; mutual accountability 6; non-OECD 12n1; *pannier commun* ('community basket') 52–3; Paris Declaration on Aid Effectiveness 20–1; partnerships 5, 6, 8, 32, 44, 55, 79–86, 94, 100; political economy analysis (PEA) 32–3; principle-agent view 26; as sources of knowledge 52; and supranational organizations 34n3; Swedish International Development Agency (SIDA) 83
drug prices, in Burkina Faso 42

Economic Cooperation of West African States (ECOWAS), Good Practices Forum in Health 29–30
economics, influence on development 96
economists, role in policymaking 22
Enhanced Structural Adjustment Facility 7

epistemic communities 22, 34n1, 96–7, 99, 111; donors 76–8; and international development 24; interpretation 22–3; push for ownership 23–4
Escobar, Arturo 19, 20
Esteva, Gustavo 19, 103
European Union (EU) 29
evidence-driven development 110
experts: donors as 10, 11, 76, 96, 98, 111; epistemic communities 22

factor for case selection, geography as 35n6
family planning 102, 103–4; and ownership 57–62
Ferguson, James 17, 92
financing, Medium-Term Expenditure Frameworks (MTEFs) 7–8
Fisher, J. 32
foreign aid 5, 18, 21; country ownership 26; donors 10; ideational elements 21–4; OECD fora on 5–6; ownership 17; Paris Declaration on Aid Effectiveness 20–1, 85; principles for improving effectiveness of 6; and uncertainty 22; *see also* Paris Declaration on Aid Effectiveness
funding, harmonization 6

GAVI Vaccinations 53
Ghana 27; ownership in 25
Global Alliance for Vaccines and Immunizations (GAVI) 100
Global Fund to Fight AIDS, Malaria, and Tuberculosis 100
global poverty 99
"going back" 120–1
good governance 70
governance 18
governments 9, 11, 12; definition of ownership 46–7; mutual accountability 6; Sector Wide Approaches (SWAps) 8
gross national income (GNI) 43
Grovugui, Siba 119

Haas, Peter 22, 24
Hall, Stuart 8

harmonization 6, 21, 26, 85
health sector 30–1; Abuja Declaration
43; Bamako Initiative (BI) 42, 43;
community-based organizations
(CBOs) 3; donor influence 54–7;
family planning 57–61, 103–4;
financial impact of donors on 101–2;
HENNET Kenya 74–6; indicators
51–2; knowledge production in 31;
non-governmental organizations
(NGOs) 79
Heavily Indebted Poor Country (HIPC)
funds 43, 69, 101
hegemonic definition of ownership 106
HENNET Kenya 74–6
homegrown development 8–9
Hountondji, Paulin 122

indigenous knowledge 35n9
influence of donors 54–7
institutionalization 22–3; of donors 78
interim PRSPs 7, 69
international aid 4
International Conference on Population
Development (ICPD) 29
international development 43; and
epistemic communities 24
international donors 42; influence of
54–7
international finance institutions (IFIs) 21
International Monetary Fund (IMF) 5,
7, 69, 101, 107, 108; loans to Kenya
82; structural adjustment programs
(SAPs) 104
interpretation 22–3
interviews: in Burkina Faso 41; in
Kenya 68

Japanese International Cooperation
Agency (JICA) 29, 74, 77, 97

Kenya 2, 3, 8, 12, 20, 21, 24, 28, 30,
33, 35n6, 67, 92; accountability
80–1; ambiguity in ownership
of development 72; civil society
88n9, 118; civil society actors 10;
civil society involvement in the
ownership process 74–6; civil
society organizations (CSOs)
95; commitment to MDGs

79; development partners 94;
Development Partnership Forum
Meetings (DPFs) 83; donor
involvement in the ownership
process 73–4; donor longevity
78–80; donors 81, 84, 93–4; donors
as epistemic community 76–8;
Economic Recovery Strategy for
Wealth and Employment Creation
(ERSWEC) 69–70; education
sector in 35n8; fieldwork in 28–9;
global health initiatives 100;
good governance 70; government
involvement in the ownership
process 72–3; health policy 100;
health sector 67, 97; health sector
funding 79; HENNET Kenya
74–6; implementation of SAPs 82;
interim PRSP 69; interviews in 68;
investment in ownership principles
81–2; Japanese International
Cooperation Agency (JICA) 97; lack
of trust between government and
donors 73–4, 85–6; loans to 69, 82;
local actors 93; market approach to
development 105; Medium-Term
Expenditure Framework (MTEF)
70; Millennium Development Goals
(MDGs) 100; Moi regime 107;
National Health Sector Strategic
Plan (NHSSP) 70; National Poverty
Eradication Plan (NPEP) 105;
National Rainbow Coalition (NARC)
69; NHSSP II 71; *nyayo* development
107; ownership in 19, 20, 67, 76,
109–10, 120; participation and
stakeholders 71–2; partnerships
100; policy-makers 100; politics
in 111; population control policies
122n1; Poverty Reduction Strategy
Paper (PRSP) 69–70, 71–2, 80,
105; Pre-Development Partnership
Forum Meetings 83; responsibility
for policy outcomes 102–3; scientific
capitalism 18; stakeholders 118;
structural adjustment programs
(SAPs) 85–6, 104; Swedish
International Development Agency
(SIDA) 83; underdevelopment in
103–6, 111, 118; Vision 2030 93

Kenya Vision 2030 70
Kenyan Education Sector Support
    Programme (KESSP) 68
Kenyatta, Jomo 109
Khan, M., on ownership 26
Kibaki, Mwai 69
Kim, Jim Yong 6–7
knowledge 61; consensual 117; donors
    as epistemic community 76–8, 96–7;
    donors as sources of 52; technical 98
knowledge production 11, 21; in
    the health sector 31; and political
    economy analysis (PEA) 32–3

*La lettre d'intention de politique de
    développement humain durable*
    ('Letter of Intent on Sustainable
    Human Development Policy'
    (LIPDHD)) 43
*La stratégie de croissance accélérée
    et de développement durable* ('The
    Strategy for Accelerated Growth
    and Sustainable Development'
    (SCADD)) 44, 52, 57
Lagos Plan of Action 123n3
l'appropriation de développement 41
l'appropriation nationale 44
*Le Cadre stratégique de lutte contre la
    pauvreté* 43
loans, to Kenya 69, 82; *see also*
    International Monetary Fund (IMF);
    World Bank
local actors 19, 21, 34, 93
long-term development strategies 7, 44,
    93, 101, 105, 110
Lumumba, Patrice 123n4

Mali, ownership in 25
Matua, Makua 120–1
McNamara, Robert 4
Medium-Term Expenditure
    Frameworks (MTEFs) 7–8, 93, 117;
    in Kenya 70
Mill, John Stuart 27
Millennium Challenge Accounts
    (MCA) 5
Millennium Development Goals
    (MDGs) 5–6 24, 29, 43, 59, 61,
    67, 93, 98, 100, 117; Kenya's
    commitment to 79

Mkandawire, Thandika 21, 25
Moi, Daniel Arap 20, 106, 108
monitoring function of CSOs 74
Monterrey Consensus 5–6, 7
movements, in Burkina Faso 47–8
moving beyond ownership 122
Mozambique, ownership in 25
Multi-County AIDS Programme
    (MAP) 100
multilateral donors 34–5n5, 56, 100
mutual accountability 6, 18

national development, *l'appropriation
    nationale* 44
*National Family Planning Stimulus
    Plan 2013–2015* 60
National Rainbow Coalition (NARC) 69
neoliberalism 5, 7, 30–1, 42, 43, 44,
    50, 72, 103, 107–8, 109, 110, 122;
    Bamako Initiative (BI) 42
NKrumah, Kwame 4
non-governmental organizations
    (NGOs) 3, 10, 17, 29, 30, 52,
    79, 84, 101–2; definition of
    ownership 75; HENNET Kenya
    74–6; *Renforcement de Capacités*
    (RENCAP) 52–3
nyayo development 107, 109
Nyerere, Julius 4

OECD Development Assistance
    Committee (OECD-DAC) 2
Organization for Economic
    Co-operation and Development
    (OECD) 1, 7, 25, 33, 93, 101,
    106; definition of ownership 2,
    116–17; fora on foreign aid 5–6;
    measurement for ownership 95
overpopulation 60–1
ownership 1–8, 10, 17, 19, 20, 24,
    25, 27, 34, 45, 61, 68–9, 75, 86–7,
    92–3, 104, 106, 116, 117, 122; and
    accountability 80–1; accountability
    118–19; Accra Agenda for Action
    (AAA) 6; ambiguity of 72; Booth on
    26; in Burkina Faso 41, 50, 110; case
    selection 29–31; in civil society 18;
    civil society organizations (CSOs)
    28; coloniality 17; consolidation of
    the language of 93–5; and decolonial

theory 11; decolonizing 121, 122; dependency embedded in 122; discourses 8, 19, 30; and donor-government relations 25; donors 26; donors' definition of 45–6; and family planning 57–61; government definition of 46–7; hegemonic definition of 106; Hillary Clinton on 16; and homegrown strategies 8–9; in Kenya 20, 67, 109–10; in the Kenyan context 76; Kenyan donor involvement in 73–4; Kenyan government involvement in 72–3; Kenya's investment in 81–2; moving beyond 122; OECD definition of 2; OECD's formal measure for 95; as a paradigm 8; as paradigm 12n3; political economy analysis (PEA) 31–3; Poverty Reduction Strategy Papers (PRSPs) 5; putative definition of 105; and sovereignty 27; stakeholders 9, 118; and the state 9

pannier commun ('community basket') 52–3
paradigms 12n3
Paris Declaration on Aid Effectiveness 5–6, 20, 68, 72, 85, 87, 92, 93–4, 97, 98, 99–100, 105, 117
Partners in Development 4
partnerships 50, 55, 58, 79–86, 94
Peace Corps 4
Pearson Commission on International Development 4
policy papers 97
policy-making 24; in Burkina Faso 100; donors as epistemic community 76–8; epistemic communities 22; interpretation 22–3; role of economists in 22
political economy analysis (PEA) 31–3
politics 111
population control policies 122n1
postcolonial movement 17
poverty reduction 5; National Poverty Eradication Plan (NPEP) 105; *see also* Poverty Reduction Strategy Papers (PRSPs)
Poverty Reduction and Growth Facility 7

Poverty Reduction Strategy Papers (PRSPs) 5, 7, 43, 55–7, 69, 80, 93, 99, 101, 117, 122; in Burkina Faso 50–1; consensual knowledge 117; *Le Cadre stratégique de lutte contre la pauvreté* 43
power 2, 18, 33, 52, 92; and coloniality 17; consensual knowledge 22; discourses 8; of epistemic communities 23
President's Emergency Plan for AIDS Relief (PEPFAR) 100
principle-agent view of ownership 26
principles for improving effectiveness of foreign aid 6
private pharmacy depots 42
professionalization 3, 23; community-based organizations (CBOs) 3–4
Programme d'Appui au Développement Sanitaire (PADS) 48, 52–4, 58–9, 103
Programme Populaire de Développement ('People's Development Program' (PPD)) 43
projects, harmonization 6
putative definition of ownership 105

Quijano, A. 17

re-legitimization, of the World Bank 93
Renforcement de Capacités (RENCAP) 52–3
resource extraction in Africa 119
responsibility for policy outcomes 102–3
results 6
Rome Declaration on Harmonization 5–6

Sankara, Thomas 20, 41, 50, 121; approach to development 107–8, 110
scientific capitalism 17–18, 19, 62, 95–9
Sector Wide Approaches (SWAps) 7, 8, 74, 80, 93, 117, 122
self-reliant development 20, 108–9
Sharma, S., on ownership 26
sovereignty 27
stakeholders 8, 9, 18, 20, 118; civil society organizations (CSOs) 9–10; in Kenya's development 71–2; local 21, 34; and scientific capitalism 18

state, the 7; African 9; and ownership 9; sovereignty 27
state-led development 4
structural adjustment programs (SAPs) 42, 85–6, 96, 104, 110; in Burkina Faso 106, 108; Kenya's implementation of 82
structural adjustments 20
Sub-Saharan Africa, state-led development in 4
supranational organizations 34n3
sustainable development 24
Sustainable Development Goals (SDGs) 16, 29, 93, 117
Swedish International Development Agency (SIDA) 83

Taylor, Ian 119
technical expertise 20, 77, 97
Third World 4
top-down development 45
transparency 6

uncertainty 22, 23, 98
underdevelopment 103–6, 111, 118, 119; in Burkina Faso 50–2
UNICEF 42
United Nations Development Programme (UNDP) 16, 20, 97
United Nations Economic Commission for Africa (UNECA) 9
United Nations Population Fund (UNFPA) 29, 94
United Nations (UN): on Africa's failure to industrialize 2; International Conference on Financing for Development 5; Millennium Development Goals (MDGs) 5; Sustainable Development Goals (SDGs) 16
universal development models 117
U.S. Agency for International Development (USAID) 5, 29, 30, 45, 55, 85, 97; Country Development Cooperation Strategy for Kenya 2014–2018 78; off-budget funding 102

Vision 2020 93
Vision 2030 93

Wolfensohn, James 98, 99, 116, 120
World Bank 4, 7, 20, 22, 29, 43, 45, 69, 74, 76–7, 81, 83, 87, 95, 97, 101, 106–8, 120, 122; adjustment loans 5; Comprehensive Development Framework (CDF) 5, 98, 99; as knowledge bank 24; loans to Kenya 82; Multi-County AIDS Programme (MAP) 100; Poverty Reduction Strategy Papers (PRSPs) 7; re-legitimization of 93; structural adjustment programs (SAPs) 104
World Food Program 55
World Health Organization (WHO) 42, 55, 97

Yanguas, Pablo, *Why We Lie About Aid* 10–11

For Product Safety Concerns and Information please contact our EU
representative GPSR@taylorandfrancis.com
Taylor & Francis Verlag GmbH, Kaufingerstraße 24, 80331 München, Germany